THE INTIMATE DIARY OF A RUSSIAN WOMAN

My Search for Meaning in the Midst of My Country's Upheaval

ELENA SUKHORUKIKH ROMINE

TRANSLATED BY ANTONINA W. BOUIS

WILLIAM MORROW AND COMPANY, INC.
NEW YORK

It is the policy of William Morrow and Company, Inc., and its imprints and affili-
ates, recognizing the importance of preserving what has been written, to print the
books we publish on acid-free paper, and we exert our best efforts to that end.

Library of Congress Cataloging-in-Publication Data

Romine, Elena.
   [Intimnyĭ dnevnik russkoi zhenshchiny. English]
   The intimate diary of a Russian woman : my search for meaning in
the midst of my country's upheaval / Elena Romine ; translated by
Antonina W. Bouis.
    p.   cm.
   Translation of: Intimnyĭ dnevnik russkoi zhenshchiny.
   ISBN 0-688-10416-9
   1. Romine, Elena. 2. Soviet Union—Politics and government—   1985—
3. Women—Soviet Union—Biography. I. Title.
DK290.3.R66A3   1992
947.085'4'092—dc20   91-42487
                                                              CIP

Printed in the United States of America

First Edition

1 2 3 4 5 6 7 8 9 10

BOOK DESIGN BY BARBARA COHEN ARONICA

Dedicated to my parents
and to my husband, Joe

Foreword

Everything in this diary is true, but it is the truth as seen through my eyes. Some facts from my life and the lives of my friends and acquaintances have been combined or shifted in time out of ethical considerations. Many names have been changed. The one episode that is related with complete documentary accuracy is the meeting with Andrei Dmitrievich Sakharov.

My diary would not have appeared without the friends with whom we were fortunate to have lived until we could write about our lives openly. I am sorry that my father did not live to see it happen.

I want to thank all those who helped and supported the creation of this book: my husband, Joe, Della van Heyst, Yuri Sorokin, and Robert Baensch.

Contents

THE
INTIMATE
DIARY OF A
RUSSIAN
WOMAN

CHAPTER ONE

Something Confused, but Which I Find Interesting

JUNE 1, 1988. The desired but inaccessible Munich and the provincial Kaluga, now in the past. Two different worlds, connected in a real way by my life. Now, as I sit in the kitchen of my Moscow apartment, I could get a phone call both from Kaluga or from Munich, although Munich is more likely.

Kaluga—my childhood at my grandparents' house—represents the time connecting me to the past, a time dear to my father. Now my father is gone, and I am the only one who would want to or, for that matter, be able to write about it.

That past is inseparable from me. I feel its presence always, that special sensation of objects, smells, light, and shadow—that is, the things that are hard to describe. But I will try nevertheless.

In my lifetime I've had several apartments, but none can compare with Kaluga. The other apartments didn't have hidden corners, special odors, or a clutter of old things that lived their own lives. I don't even remember how the furniture was placed in the later apartments. But I don't need any effort to recall the Kaluga apartment; I could walk through it with my eyes shut.

The magic of that house began far outside its big, heavy gates. The name of the street—Pushkinskaya—spoke with its soft sounds of another century, which was recollected on every intersection of Kaluga. The house did not sit at the corner; it was set back from it near Store No. 6, a completely modern store since its shelves were almost always bare. The building "stretched out" to the city park and the Suburban Garden. The long street, which changed its name several times, led to three memorable spots: the city park, the Stone Bridge, and the ravine. The windows of my great-grandfather's study opened onto the park. He was chief of the Kaluga section of the railroad. Those windows were like an ellipsis at the beginning of Grandfather's stories about his travels with his father in a separate railroad car that was like an apartment. You could come back to our building across the Stone Bridge. It spanned a large ravine, which, I believe, held a chapel over a sacred spring. People said that the ravine was dangerous, that robbers capable of murder hid in the thick bushes, but I was attracted by it. I wanted to look down into the bushes despite the danger.

The road was uneven—with hills and bumps. On one rise stood a private house with large wrought-iron lampposts at the entrance, a nobleman's house. Fate had turned it into a regional studies museum. Farther down, three streets met. One led to our house, another looped around sharply down to the Oka River, and the third ended at St. George's Church, where we all had been baptized and which we attended on holidays. Around the corner from the church was the house where my grandfather had been born, a house that reminded him of his mother's early death and of his capricious and egotistical stepmother. It was called the Goncharov house by St. George's. Apparently its original owners were the Goncharovs.

At the beginning of Pushkinskaya Street was a Soyuzpechat newspaper kiosk. It used to be a chapel of a church that was razed in the thirties. My father and uncle had gone to church there for Easter services. They would be awakened in the middle of the night, dressed in their sailor suits, and then make their way mysteriously through the festive darkness. On the left side of the street stood a large red building, the "home for little ones." I was horrified by the very idea. How could anyone live without parents and grandparents!

JULY 3. I've been in a horrible mood, which has made me feel weak, and I'm not much better, even now. I've discovered a new, marvelous masochistic leitmotiv: my ruined life. It shimmers with new shades every day. Mixing with the alarm that comes externally (from books, newspapers, magazines, the television, and people), my anxiety grows to universal proportions. The leitmotiv has many smaller motivs running through it: I'm a poorly educated person; I don't know how to do anything well; I'm tired of lying and playing at working. Everything irritates me; from sounds and smells to my inability to solve the simplest problems in my life. My personal life is a shambles; the ones I want to see are far away, and the rest I don't care about. How do I get out of this circle? Depend on Fazil Iskander's understanding of the sense of humor—the trail you leave behind as you climb out of the abyss? This mood brings with it unexpected physical sensations. Yesterday I was in a restaurant with friends, and at the next table some guy dumped black and red caviar into his plate and mixed them together. I still can't shake the revulsion I felt at the sight of that mixture. Maybe it was the dream I had in which I ate a nauseating black and red sweet-tasting mush. My doctor would probably blame my liver or ask if I was pregnant. Whatever the explanation, I feel vile.

JULY 5. Is it possible to be completely frank? I'll try. What am I afraid of in life? The death of family (I have only my mother left), heights (I get dizzy and sick), enclosed spaces (a subway car or an elevator if it stops unexpectedly), pain (that's normal), crowds (ever since childhood, when we were trapped in one near the subway on a holiday), metal constructions (especially if covered with soot and dirt), the thought that someone might attack me or get into the apartment through the balcony. And I'm afraid of steps. That's my Yalta disease. I had been waked at night to come to the phone at the resort hotel. My mother hadn't been able to get through to my room, and she called the desk and asked someone to get me. Someone did. Sleepy, I ran down the stairs. I didn't fall, but the sense of running and sliding half asleep is with me today, even when I make my way firmly and cautiously down the stairs. I began thinking about fears and realized that I have too many. Even the movement of my beloved turtle in its box can startle me into spasms of fear.

Of course, most of my fears go back to my childhood. Then they were related to secrets and childish fantasies rather than to actual danger. There was a toilet set up in the corner of the kitchen in our Kaluga apartment, and I had to muster all my courage to go there at night. I had to cross the small entry to reach it, and the front door was there. What if someone opened the door and came in? I was afraid of the little window near the kitchen ceiling that our cats used in order to come in and out.

What if some goblin used it instead? From the living-room windows I could see the attic of the house next door, where, according to the neighborhood kids, a deathly pale hand emerged and waved. At night a monstrous face might peer into our windows that opened on the street. I wasn't afraid in the bedroom. Grandmother shut the heavy curtains tightly and lit the votive light beneath the icon of St. Nicholas, the miracle worker.

The childish fear of death tormented me, too. A small yard had miraculously survived in front of our house. The branches of two American maples hung over a wooden table and benches. A paper lantern was suspended over the table. We drew, played cards, had tea, and sometimes ate meals there. Moths circled the lantern on warm summer evenings and beat their wings against the bright lamp. An adult remarked that moths lived only twenty-four hours. We didn't believe it, discussed it for a long time, and then forgot it as something unpleasant and therefore unnecessary.

JULY 9. There are two ways to survive in Moscow: either take up a deeply defensive position, reducing forays into the world to a minimum, or become a biofeedback virtuoso. Otherwise you are doomed or turned into a constant victim of lines and the accompanying squabbles they engender. I stick to the first tactic; my nerves aren't the best. Unfortunately staying home isn't always possible. Today I left the house to get my shoes repaired and pick up some groceries—bread, milk, and butter. There was a long line at the shoe repair shop, with only one

clerk accepting and returning shoes as well as placing the finished work on the shelves. There was something mystical about
the whole process. The shoes were always found, but locating
each pair took almost seven minutes. The line waited patiently.
My biofeedback didn't work, and I began to boil over. My first
desire was to tell all of them in the line that they were stupid
sheep and shouldn't allow themselves to be treated this way.
But you need a partner for scenes like this. Recently Olya (small
and fragile but with an explosive temper) and I had made a
scene. It was rather funny. Someone in the crowd responded
that "this was better than being under the Germans." We expressed our doubts and gave figures on the number of people
leaving for Germany. But Olya wasn't with me today, so I waited
patiently. I did have a small scene anyway because the woman
behind me decided "to straighten things out" and push me back
three places in line. But there is a higher justice after all. Her
shoes weren't accepted because the sewing machine was out of
order and the store didn't have the material for the repair. The
clerk took two pairs out of the three I brought. Incredible luck.
I felt avenged. In short, everything developed according to the
best laws of drama.

There was a second act, too, that took place in the grocery
store and was less interesting. I couldn't buy a thing, not even
milk. A customer leaving empty-handed is regarded with suspicion; maybe you stole something. My bag was checked at the
exit, and I opened it gladly: Look, I'm an honest Soviet citizen.
Then I headed for the section for special customers—people
with large families or invalids. The shelves were pretty bare
there, too, but there was butter. There had been butter in the

main section, but I would have had to stand in line for it. I asked if I could buy the butter in the special section. The two cashiers were obviously bored without work. With enviable inventiveness they suggested I return to the original line to buy several packs of butter instead of one. That way I wouldn't feel so bad about standing in line and I'd have a supply on hand.

As I write, I've thought of a third way to deal with life: a sense of humor. For some reason I have trouble managing that. It keeps slipping away.

JULY 14.   It turns out that it's "in" to be healthy in America. Not here yet. It is said that in America people even consider how you look when you're being hired for work. We all consider it acceptable to be sick several times a year—a flu epidemic or a cold in bad weather or exhaustion from work and worries. Very few of my women friends exercise or play sports.

As a friend of mine said, you have to decompress after work. There are two effective ways: run several kilometers or drink a bottle of vodka. Naturally he prefers the latter. My women friends don't drink vodka, but they watch TV or spend hours on the phone. It never occurs to them to go for a jog or a swim at the pool. Of course, we don't have many such opportunities. You have to spend several hours in line to buy a pool membership, and that's after checking in to get a place in line several days before that. Sports in our country are for the elite.

But laziness takes its toll too. Every so often I vow to exercise in the mornings. Two or three days later I'm making up excuses: I didn't sleep well today; tomorrow I'll exercise later in the day, it's even better for you; or I'm not in the mood, and so on. It's easy to persuade yourself. Then, however, I'm filled with scorn for my own weakness, which creates even greater stress. But I still don't reach for the vodka.

JULY 15. I always had a clear assessment of our life. I knew more than others about the past, and I had learned to understand that past properly. But now I am lost. Either the world around me seems so gloomy because of my bad mood or my mood is caused by our gloomy life. I have an equally morbid reaction to everything—first indignation, then rumination, a desire to express my attitude, a painful search for thoughts and words, and last, a sense of impotence, at overcoming my depression or understanding what is happening, at expressing myself or changing anything with my anger. And I'm not very verbal—a result of my Soviet education. But I will continue my diary, even if it's not very good and I'm not happy with it.

Today I thought that the harshness of our everyday lives deforms our personal lives. A normal sexual, spiritual, or whatever kind of relationship with a man turns into something that is not a manifestation of femininity. Soviet women have gone mad. Five minutes "after" in bed we're talking about politics. So we select only smart men as bed partners, mostly for that "afterward." From what my friends tell me, we're all doing that. Does that mean that there is no hope at all for normal love?

JULY 17. I think I'm beginning to understand the cause of my strange condition. Until recently we lived in the world of ideas, emotions, suffering—but not action. Why bustle? You can't change anything any way. But now something's started moving. It's time to wake up, but we don't know how.

It's hard and scary to start over at thirty-five. What am I worth; what haven't I forgotten how to do yet? For a while I was lying low, gathering strength, and now I'm taking my first baby steps. Tragedy left our family unscathed; no one spent time in the camps, even though by all standards someone should have. Everyone died a natural death. But fear stalked us, too. It was the fear of saying too much, the fear of meeting with foreigners, the fear of acting. It's not completely gone yet, but the fear of freedom is already here. We've forgotten how to make decisions and take hold of our own lives. I, for one, am afraid to take a wrong step. I don't have time for mistakes. I'll never make up what I've lost as it is. On the other hand, Father's death freed me of many fears.

What a mix my diary is. But man is a mix. So who am I? Medium height, not badly built. Hair darker than blond, with straight bangs to the brows. Rather large features; animation bordering on nervousness. Good white teeth still, which allow me to smile often and with pleasure (I'm told my smile looks good). I try to dress either elegantly or sportily, depending on my mood. I pay attention to color combinations. I like jewelry in moderation. On the whole I tend to dress conservatively. Extravagant clothing requires intense behavior, which tires me. I have rather beautiful hands, and I use them boldly in conversation. The freedom of my gestures and movements depends on my mood. My attitude toward my looks varies. Sometimes I see an attractive woman in the mirror, and other times someone who's almost ugly. I think that God gave me a reasonable amount of looks that allow me to live in harmony with my inner sensations.

JULY 18. I had a strange dream last night. I was walking through rooms with some people. Ahead was a man I knew was Stalin. In a room with light gray walls were tables holding light gray machines—instruments of torture. I realized what was about to happen to us. I ran and found myself in a large, airy vestibule, and I hid in a doorway. I was safe; no one saw me. I went down a broad staircase. At the building entrance I was approached by a young woman, I think a Bulgarian. We decided that we couldn't go home. "They" could be waiting for us there. We walked along a line of houses beyond which was a beach. We undressed and got into the water. For a long time we swam with great pleasure. Then a huge wave came, threatening to engulf us. Where did it go? We were safe.

I dreamed of a threatening gigantic wave last year. Mother and I were swimming in the open sea. It was dark. Heavy water hung over us. It looked as if we would die, but we saw the lights of a big city with skyscrapers. It was New York. We calmly swam to shore and came out on a sandy beach. A miracle or clairvoyance?

JULY 20. And so our trip to Kaluga came to pass. My most horrible and tormenting moments were not at the cemetery. It was strange even for me that I felt good and at peace there; my tears were almost not bitter. Father's whole family had gathered there. They were no longer threatened by any misfortune, and they were surrounded by the graves of people they had loved in life. Old Kaluga, scattered in little islands throughout a city that has retained almost nothing but the name, is alive at the cemetery. Everything is still the same at our old St. George's Church, thank God, but now it is connected with the funerals of Grandfather and Father more than with my childhood. We found only fragments of the old life on Pushkinskaya Street. The street is now called Korolyov. The gates are gone, as is our small front yard. The courtyard is open to the whole street, along which huge trucks race. In the past there was a trolley with its soothing and familiar sound every fifteen minutes or so. At the back of the courtyard stand the remains of the sheds where we stored wood and other household necessities and kept some chickens. There I tried to smoke for the first time with Seryozha, a boy from our block. We ate sprats to kill the tobacco smell, and our hands stank from them. The trash bin, which the garbage men emptied regularly, is gone. We used to call the garbage men pilots, probably in sarcastic contrast since being a pilot was considered very romantic.

A vile old woman and her mad daughter live in our former house. They wouldn't let me in. Maybe that was for the best. I managed to peek in through the mail slot and saw the wall of the main entrance. The boards are still painted light blue, but the padding on the door is ragged. That was when I really cried.

I saw some of the old neighbors. They have such horrible,

joyless lives. All that's left of the past is the life that destroys
human dignity: a huge, filthy kitchen for a dozen families; an
antediluvian sink with no hot water; dark hallways leading to
cell-like rooms. In the past this pathetic communal life was made
more pleasant by the shared life of the courtyard. We had our
own singer and our poet and the hardest-drinking drunk and
the best skittles player. My grandparents told me what it had
been like even before that. Among the inhabitants of the houses
that opened on the inner courtyard were a general and a priest,
a helpless blind old man who was shot by the Bolsheviks. Now
fat, frowsy women wander in the courtyard. One woman's son
drove up in his car. He was still young, but he had already lost
all his teeth. We talked about those who had died, who had
become drunkards, who had served their time, and who were
still inside.

JULY 21. I have my passport and my visa and money in my
wallet. All I have to do is pack and get on the plane. I've been
waiting for this for the last four years, actually for my whole life,
and now I definitely don't want to go to Munich. I want to go
to Paris. This is too much, I tell myself. By Soviet standards this
isn't merely snobbery; it's total moral corruption: I don't want
Munich; I want Paris. There's a simple explanation: I need J-P.
I haven't wanted anything serious, for Wolfgang is waiting for
me in Munich, and our two-month-long telephone affair is going
to begin for real. And now I'm completely confused. A million
versions whiz through my brain: I go to Munich and from there
to Paris; I get to Munich, meet J-P, and then I don't know what;

I don't go anywhere and wait for J-P in Moscow. I'm going crazy. I've lost several pounds; I can't eat; I just cry. Besides, J-P has vanished. He hasn't called in several days. And I thought that I'd never be stupid again, that it was all behind me. Yet every time it's the same thing: This is the real thing, and all the rest has merely been a preparation for him.

JULY 26. Things are still unclear in Paris. So I'm going to Munich, going to Wolfgang, and giving myself up to fate. I'm trying not to think about anything. I don't have the strength.

CHAPTER TWO

Moscow–Munich–Moscow, or My First Trip to the West as a Free Person

Your betrayal suits her more than caresses.
Do not forget, as you press her to your chest,
That she will tell all that you are
For as many years as there are ahead.
—BELLA AKHMADULINA

JULY 30. Apparently I have the strength not only to pack but to go to the beauty parlor and pull myself together, and once again I want to go to Munich.

All the customs and passport procedures went amazingly quickly. It was even boring. I wanted obstacles; it's the first time I'm going to the West without an accompanying eye.

The plane takes off, and I cry, an unoriginal thought coming to mind. Neil Armstrong said that a small step for man was an enormous step for mankind. And I'm thinking that a small step for mankind (only a few thousand kilometers) is an enormous step in my life. This is my first trip to the free world as a free person. Before this I traveled to Eastern Europe and on typical Soviet tours to the Mediterranean and to India. I'm experiencing a mix of triumphant and sentimental, sorrowful and joyous feelings. And wild curiosity—what will I see? As usual, anticipation is always stronger and sweeter than the moment of arrival.

JULY 31.   I was bewildered by the airport—so many passage-ways, escalators, halls. Following the crowd, I got ready for my meeting with Wolfgang. He must not see me confused and frightened. I prepared an American smile on my face, exhausted by Soviet worries. I picked up my suitcases and waited.

Wolfgang appeared in my life in April. Late one evening the telephone rang, and my old pal Peter said that he was calling from Munich and that he had a friend with him who was inviting me to spend my vacation in Germany. Of course, this kind gesture had been prompted by Peter, who knew how much I wanted to go there. A few days later there was another call, this time from Wolfgang. He asked me to send a letter with my photograph and to tell him a little about myself. His calls gradu-ally became more frequent and eventually became daily. We began the classic romance by letter of the soldier in the Soviet army, but this was the foreign version: calls between Moscow and Munich instead of mail between Pribalkalye and Kostroma. Soon he had persuaded himself that he was practically in love with me, and more interestingly, I had done the same. I liked talking with him on the phone. I liked his voice, his frankness, and his obvious interest in me. His photograph, which came a few weeks later, made me wary. He was too handsome and looked too young to be forty-two. But the photograph did not interrupt our telephone romance. I think we even set a record for the *Guinness Book of World Records*: the longest telephone conversation between Munich and Moscow—three and a half hours. Too bad no one could register it.

That evening a friend had tried and tried to call me. She later said that she thought I was probably making love by phone. That was almost true. The phone was by the bed, and the calls often came at one or two in the morning. In July Wolfgang flew to New York, and J-P arrived in Moscow. . . .

I searched for Wolfgang in the crowd. There he was, looking like his picture, but older and somehow different. I think he was also bewildered and frightened—so many words and promises. What if he had rushed things? But now we had no choice. There I was. I set my suitcases on the floor and hugged and kissed a man who was practically a stranger. There was no time to think about what I was feeling. I was in Germany. Here it was—wide autobahns, small roadside cafés that have everything your heart could desire, ancient cities with churches, flowers everywhere, and once more the road through tended fields, small woods, and hills. I forgot to say that I had landed in Frankfurt. I couldn't get a ticket to Munich.

There didn't seem to be love at first, or second, sight, but there was no sense of disliking either. At last we were in Munich, walking around the city. It's cozy, calm, a bit provincial, and not in the least foreign. I think I'll like it here.

AUGUST 3. I wasn't mistaken. I like it in Munich. First of all, I'm growing accustomed to the sense of physical comfort I already knew from East Germany. No one shoves me; I don't have to be prepared to fight back. The cafés and toilets don't have that horrible Soviet smell. You can eat, sit down and rest, drop into a store any time and place you want; you can see an illustration of that "radiant future" which I have been "building" along with my compatriots. I'm trying not to stuff myself with architectural and artistic values. I'm wandering around the city, looking at the passersby, at the store windows. Marienplatz and the surrounding streets are a tourist's joy. You can spend day after day there without tiring. And all my independent trips around the city start and end there for now.

But I'm not one to be calm and happy if there's an excuse to do a little suffering. My relations with Wolfgang are strange— both good and not good. I can't really tell yet. A romance should be developing, but it's not. Our relationship resembles what usually comes after an affair. Maybe it is the fault of our "telephone love."

AUGUST 5. For a Soviet, "abroad" and "border" have special connotations. "Going abroad," "being allowed abroad," "crossing the border" are signs of something unusual. I can't refuse myself this "being abroad" game, even though my desire to spend ten minutes on Austrian soil and have a cup of coffee in a roadside café may seem strange. Peter understands me because at one point a risky crossing of the border changed his entire life. Once he found himself in the "other" Germany. He patiently tried to persuade the border guards to let his "American girl friend" who had forgotten her passport back at the hotel come into Austria with him. I nodded and used a few English words. As it turns out, we could have driven across the border without a passport. They rarely check. The coffee was like coffee anywhere, and the Austrians aren't any different from the Germans, but at least I'll have a story to tell back home. After all, I can't tell them about how beautiful it is in the Alps and how marvelous views from the mountain roads are. I don't have the eloquence for that.

But I can't resist showing off to my mother. "I'm calling you from a phone booth by the road. I'm surrounded by the Alps. It's rather nice." She can't see the Alps from her small Moscow apartment, but she was happy for me.

AUGUST 7. Wolfgang is glum and silent and says it has to do with his worries. I'd like to believe that, but I can't. At last we had it out. One evening he went out (for a bit!) and didn't come back for more than a day. It turned out that a few days before he left for New York he had fallen in love with a girl who was sharing his apartment until her own became available. He ran into her and realized that he was still in love with her. In revenge, I tell him about J-P. We end up trying to call Paris at two in the morning, and I fall asleep at dawn.

AUGUST 9. J-P called at last. He'll probably come to Munich soon. So now I have to wait. How do I fill the time?

First of all, you can't get away from Russia. I called up Yury K., a poet exiled from the Soviet Union seven years ago. The three of us (his daughter came from Moscow) wandered around town. Even though he is a young and contemporary man, there is something of the traditional Russian émigré about him: his manner of speech, his gait, if nothing else his walking stick umbrella. We tossed around Moscow problems and emotions on the cozy streets of Munich. From here they seemed bittersweet. His attentiveness prompted me to tell him everything about my life. There's more space for Russian speech here than at home. It's strange or, more precisely, unfair. We went to the Alte Pinakotech, had some German beer, and then looked at the paintings.

I told Wolfgang about our day that evening. He listened closely, but I don't think he understands half of what I was talking about. How can I tell him about an exiled Russian poet when he has no feel for or interest in poetry?

AUGUST 12. One of the most attractive spots in Munich is the English Garden. Radio Liberty, one of the most important and inseparable parts of my Moscow life, is located there. The building is disappointingly ordinary, just a few low houses behind a fence. I had thought . . . On Sunday I went to the park nevertheless and found a large open-air beer hall: gigantic mugs of beer, substantial German food, and peaceful faces happy with life. I sat down at a table with a mug of beer and started up a sociable conversation with my neighbor, a merry and friendly Bavarian. Suddenly I felt a sharp pain in my hand: a wasp or bee sting. Actually it was nice to feel a little sorry for myself. But by the next day things took a more serious turn. My hand was swollen, I couldn't even bend my fingers, and Wolfgang and I had been planning a trip to Hamburg. We went to a doctor. That was almost like an excursion to a museum for me, and it turned out to be much more interesting. The museums here are like our museums, while the doctors are completely different and much better. This doctor was charming, unhurried, and amiable, as if we had come to visit him at home. Talk about my hand was interspersed with other conversation. Even the shot, which usually terrifies me, was not bad. While the doctor unpacked the syringe, filled it with medication, and painlessly injected it into my vein, I told him about our problems with AIDS and other infections caused by dirty needles. Wolfgang and the doctor were surprised. They could barely believe it. They sympathized. The doctor didn't want to be paid—it's not every day he has a Russian patient—but Wolfgang insisted.

AUGUST 14. "Hamburg" always brings to mind corruption and vice—a port! But it's nothing of the sort; it's an ordinary city. While Wolfgang looked for an inexpensive hotel, I looked out the car window at a woman strolling up and down on the sidewalk, trying to see any "signs" that she was prostitute. To my disappointment, she didn't try to pick anyone up. She merely smoked nervously. *Things must be bad with customers*, I thought.

I don't know about customers, but things certainly looked bad for vice on famous Reeperbahn. The sex shops were almost empty, and the shills tried to lure even me into the video salons. Apparently my curious gaze made them think I was interested. I quickly finished with the life of sin and went off to see the architectural sights. Hamburg seemed cold and distant after Munich, despite the incredible heat that day, which almost killed me by evening. Wolfgang was late for our appointment, and I spent three hours hanging around the station entrance. Not the best place to wait! At least I learned how men try to pick up women in this city, although the men weren't German and not even European. Several attempts were made, and they all began with inhuman patience. First the men stared at me for a half hour. Then they came over and offered to help. One asked for a lighter, even though I wasn't smoking. Not very inventive! But he was the one I almost asked for help. I suddenly realized that I was going to pass out from the heat and my exhaustion. That had never happened to me before, and I panicked. Still, I decided not to depend on a dubious helper and went inside the station to look for the first-aid room. Luckily things went well. One of the waiting rooms was air-conditioned, and I felt better.

What was I to do if Wolfgang didn't show up? Even though I knew it was unlikely, I decided to work through the situation, just in case. It was getting toward evening. First I said to myself, "You can't handle this simple situation. Go back to your quiet socialist paradise." That set me straight. I found a few ways out: buy a ticket home (which is how I regarded Munich by now) or get a room in a hotel and then call Wolfgang's office in the morning. I counted my money. I had enough for a hotel, but what about the ticket? I decided to wait until eight and then think about the ticket. And just then Wolfgang showed up as calm as could be. I didn't make a scene or rebuke him! I calmly said, "A little more, and I would have fainted. Or maybe died."

After a delicious dinner and big mug of beer, we sped back to Munich to the music of the Kleiderman orchestra (Wolfgang bought me a cassette in the roadside café). It was raining, and the sky was filled with dark gray, heavy clouds, through which the full moon shone. "I have the feeling that we're racing from our lives into nothingness," I said to Wolfgang.

"We're simply driving fast from Hamburg to Munich," he replied. But you can't stop me that easily.

"I've come up with a title for a short story, '*De Munich à Hambourg avec l'amour pour la lune*,' understand?"

"How can I not? I know French well."

At that moment I realized that it was a lot easier to love the moon.

AUGUST 17. I think I'm beginning to guess what's behind the cliché of the "mysterious Russian soul." We ruthlessly expend ourselves without counting on a concrete "earthly" result. It's a kind of emotional dissoluteness (or genius?). Our actions and spiritual moves have no specific goals, and as a result, there is total unpredictability. Wolfgang can't understand the reasons for my suffering. It never occurs to him to ask why. These lessons in nonunderstanding are useful for me and exhausting for him. He wants everything to be in its place. After long conversations and arguments I go into town for new impressions, while he continues arguing with his common sense. When I get back, I find letters from him, appealing to my reason.

Sometimes I infuriate him. Recently during lunch in a restaurant I said that there is no single truth, that everyone has his own. He slammed the salt shaker down onto the table and practically yelled that the sound of that shaker was an objective reality for everyone. "But everyone perceives that sound in his own way," I countered calmly.

So which of us has an easier life? Neither. He does not recognize emotions; he just keeps getting enmeshed in them and does not understand what is happening to him. Then my help can save him. I rationally analyze his irrationality, and he agrees with a smile. We switch places, and everything is mixed up. If we were in love with each other, we wouldn't need to discuss this. I'd like to see our relationship through his eyes.

And still, Wolfgang, I thank you for your common sense. I miss it so much!

AUGUST 20. "In all the time I've lived in Munich, nothing like this has ever happened to me," Wolfgang said in amazement. I was walking in Schwabing, the student section of the city, when a man came up to me and asked me something in German. When he saw that my German wasn't very good, he switched to English.

"What is your favorite color?"

"Purple," I replied without hesitation.

"Then let's go."

I didn't know why, but I followed. It didn't seem dangerous. There were lots of people around, and the sign on the door said DIANETICS CENTER. I was going to be tested and told about my problems. I had to answer 180 seemingly simple questions, and do it quickly, without thinking.

I filled out the test card without difficulty, and then a pleasant young woman discussed the results with me. I was a find for them, more problems than they knew how to handle. All my fears, confusions, and vacillations were laid bare. It was like a session of psychoanalysis. I told attentive Uta all my suffering with great pleasure. There was hope: I could take a special course, which cost around two hundred marks, and everything would fall into place. I didn't know about the course, and I didn't have a lot of money, but just having this conversation was a great relief to me. For a small sum I purchased a book about Dianetics, which the blurb says has saved many people. I asked Uta what principle of selection was used for test subjects. "If a person answers without hesitation, quickly and clearly, the way you did, it means he is open and a bit unhappy," she said. "Those are the ones we talk to and try to help."

Besides, you want my money, I thought, but that didn't reduce my gratitude for her sincere and generous attention. But it was still fantastic how well they found me—a suffering Russian soul in prosperous, tranquil, and well-balanced Munich.

I went to a café and with gusto ate a plate of fried calamari.

AUGUST 22. Hello, Erica! At last I am closer to you—in Munich now. What a long trip, though. I read your first book, *Fear of Flying*, ten years ago, and it was love from page one. And with love came envy, for your frankness of description. From you I learned courage and the ability to accept defeat, especially in my personal life, and to understand my weaknesses. When people hurt my pride, I thought of you, and it helped. And then came the desire to write about myself. No, no, I don't want to be the Soviet Erica Jong. I'm different, and my life was different.

I'm sitting in Wolfgang's kitchen and drinking Russian vodka he got as a present from Moscow. J-P won't be coming to Munich. He'll probably never come to me, ever.

Well, then, I'll light the fire, and drink.
Buying a dog might be good.

Russian poetry has many consoling words for love. I'll survive.

Now, at last, I can get to know Munich properly. I spend my days wandering the city, going to museums, sitting in beer halls and cafés.

The day of my departure draws near. Erica Jong had *Fear of Flying*. I have *Fear of Leaving*. Poor Wolfgang is going crazy. I change my mind ten times a day—leaving, staying. Reason sends me home: I have to go to work, what would I live on here, my mother is waiting for me, and so on and so forth. My weak flesh resists: I don't want to go back to my problems; I don't want to leave this comfortable life for empty stores, crowds, and the gray, dreary autumn. I realize that life is not black and white, but my subconscious reaction is stronger than I am. Au revoir, Munich, au revoir, and not farewell. Thank you for everything you taught me.

CHAPTER THREE

Divorce

And the first betrayal, there's fog at dawn.
And the second betrayal, he staggered drunk.

And the third betrayal, it's blacker than night,
Blacker than night, scarier than war.
—BULAT OKUDJAVA

SEPTEMBER 7. Today is my ex-husband's birthday. I called him at work in the morning, and the whole conversation lasted three minutes. Are we such strangers that we have nothing to talk about? Of course, he always was taciturn. I liked that at first. I thought it was a typically male trait. Then it became a burden—loneliness together.

As I later learned, our marriage was an attempt for both of us to find ourselves. He had everything: a good family; career; popularity with women. By Soviet standards, I was considered successful, too. But neither of us believed happiness was possible in this country. We wanted something more, but I tried to fight for it while he found his joy in small pleasures—television, books, a good meal. Most of all, he wanted to be left alone.

At first love (or being in love?) blinded us to everything. One night of our first month I was in bed under a heavy blanket. It was a cold winter night. He put on warm clothes and went out on the balcony. "I'm so happy that I want to die, to jump from the balcony. It won't ever be like this again," he said.

"And what if I were to die?" I replied.

"I couldn't live without you," I heard him say out on the balcony.

What was it—love, passion?

SEPTEMBER 10. His passion wasn't only for me, it turned out. I have always hated our revolutionary holidays. Everyone partied while I stayed home and felt depressed. A protest of sorts. And it was on the day the Winter Palace had been taken that my husband had his own sexual revolution: He didn't come home that night. When was it, three, four years ago? I thought he had been murdered, mugged, kidnapped. I walked up and down the street all night. I remember the red flags fluttering against one another. A Communist hell! Policemen came up to me. They thought I was stealing car parts. But after our chat they cheered up; they wished all their thieves were like me. We agreed that a nocturnal stroll was the best thing for insomnia.

He came back, guilty and hung over, around eleven the next day. He had been at a party, had too much to drink, fallen asleep, and awakened in the morning. I didn't ask, "In whose bed?" He looked so innocent and sincere.

Then it started. Every six to eight weeks he disappeared overnight, begging me not to tell anyone. His repentance was so sincere that he believed his own lies. During the sleepless nights I hated him; I waited all the time for him to come home.

I couldn't stand him anymore, but I couldn't live without him. He'd come back happy and relaxed, loving and ready to turn himself in. For the following week I had total power over him. A few weeks later he'd become repulsive, and without realizing it, I'd start waiting for the next sleepless night.

Now I know that it was a childish but very dangerous game for grown-ups. It led to indifference. I began not to care whether he came home or not.

SEPTEMBER 11. Sunday, 11:00 A.M., I just woke up, alone. Why are Saturday and Sunday the most horrible days? In the West people all wish one another a good weekend, but we don't have weekends; there's no place to go. The best thing is to run off into the woods; that's what the smart people do. But I want something special, a small holiday. Should I visit friends or go to the movies or to the theater? I spend several hours in indecision. If I have to cross town by bus and metro, I'll get hungry, and there's no place to eat; I'll get tired and come home angry. Friends talk only about politics, problems, and how lousy things are. By three in the afternoon I see that it's too late, and I almost feel relieved. There's no more issue of choice. I'll stay home, get into bed, and read. I call my friends, just in case. Maybe something's happening. No, they're depressed, too, domestic stuff. One invites me to dinner, but it's getting dark, and it's cold out. Everything seems to be in favor of staying home. It's good that I'm alone. There's no one to annoy me.

It was worse with my husband. He turned on the TV the minute he woke up. He didn't care what was on—a kiddie show, a feature on the valorous Soviet army, or gardening advice—so long as there was noise. He said it was good for his nervous system. He lay about in bed while I made breakfast. I'd get furious, a small morning exercise in hatred, and the day was ruined. Huffy looks over breakfast. Then he'd go back to the room to watch the set while I did the dishes. Dreary, dreary, dreary. And I'd spend the whole day doing chores while he'd read on the couch. I couldn't wait for Mondays!

He didn't have any friends, and we didn't visit mine very often. I never knew how he'd behave. He could be cheerful and talkative, or he could be gloomy and not say a word all evening.

Why could we stay in for days at a time in the first months of our marriage and be happy? What had happened to us? The gray monster of our grim life devoured our love.

Sometimes I'd raise a silly rebellion. I'd go off to visit friends by myself, more in order to show him and get revenge than to have fun. The revenge part didn't work. It didn't upset him. Once I came home late, tipsy, with a cake from a Georgian admirer. I immediately told him who had given me the cake. He calmly washed the dishes, seeing that I wasn't up to domestic duties. My mother later said that in his place she would have dumped the cake on my head.

SEPTEMBER 17. It's vile remembering all this, but on the other hand, it's useful, so that I don't repeat the mistakes.

Gradually I stopped being a gregarious and curious person and turned into a gloomy Soviet bitch. Instead of books, I was interested in the empty bottles piled in the kitchen, the refurbishing the apartment needed, the grocery bags. I made scenes over five rubles. In conversation I developed disgusting phrases: "cover expenses," "plaster the holes," and so on. I was cranky around the apartment, unkempt and in a robe, throwing objects around angrily. What was happening to me? At night we managed not to touch in our small bed. Often he sat up until two or three in the morning listening to the radio in the kitchen or reading American mysteries. In the mornings I hid under a pillow so as not to see and hear him go off to work. I felt he did everything wrong—eat, sleep, dress. I wonder what he thought of me.

I was intolerable at times. I had to get it off my chest. I'd start picking on him, and he kept quiet, making me crazier. I didn't stop until he started shouting. We didn't have stormy and passionate reconciliations after our fights. We were losing our love and respect for each other. Instead of moving forward, I was hurtling downward. I knew that it couldn't go on for long.

SEPTEMBER 19.   People say that we keep the good from the past and forget the bad. But all I have is the bad.

He was big, a bit fat, soft, and kind. It was pleasant kissing him. He smelled like a clean, sweet child. In bed he was silent and unrushed. He considered himself a specialist in female psychology. Maybe that's why he continued paying attention to other women: Those poor lonely females needed him. This is the good part, and I can only be sarcastic about it.

He wasn't greedy at all. When he had money, he spent it on me. The problem was that he rarely had money.

I'm back being petty and nasty about him. He was smart and educated. He was interesting to talk to, even though he often preferred silence. Soon after the wedding we stopped talking about books, art, or politics.

I'm sure that we would have made marvelous lovers or friends if we hadn't married. That's why I feared marriage for so long afterward. Marriage shows all the flaws of our system. The irritations and humiliations accumulate over the day, and pour out at home in the evening. I didn't have the nerve to talk back to my boss, to defend my position. At home we pay for our chiefs' nastiness, the low salaries, the crowded metro, the lines in the stores. Isn't it better to be alone?

SEPTEMBER 20. The wisdom of a thirty-five-year-old woman: Your worst enemy is yourself, or rather, your weakness, your egoism, and your impatience.

When we fall in love, we want it all right away. We can't stand anticipation, vagueness, tension. As a result, we ruin everything. At the start of the best romance I worried so much about a bad ending that I made it happen.

How old was I, around nineteen? Mother and I went to visit friends at the cinematographers' resort. I was walking down a path in a new dress with large blue daisies on white with red dots in the center and a white lace collar. A romantic girl with long hair. Since this is the cinematographers' place, it has to be like a movie. . . . The bushes parted, and a handsome, bearded youth, with enormous blue eyes and a charming light Georgian accent, came out. He said there was a party and invited me to join them for cake and cognac. I ran to Mother for permission. Our strict friend disappeared for ten minutes to find out who the young man was and what the party was for. He led me to the house of Georgian artists and, giving my young friend a severe look, left me there in his care. But the party was over, the cognac was gone, and we went for a walk by the lake.

He was from Tbilisi and was in Moscow with his teacher to work on his dissertation. His name was Grigol. He was elegant, shy, and mysterious. Grigol took me by taxi (a real gentleman, it's forty kilometers to town) to my friend's house. We had a date to go to the movies. I rushed into my friend's apartment and announced that I was in love.

But instead of happiness there was only torment. He wrote poetry at night and slept late. I sat by the phone waiting for his call, not eating breakfast, I couldn't swallow a thing. As soon as he called, Mother ran to warm up the food. It was an American brunch, but without the champagne, which wouldn't have hurt.

Then we spent the day in Zagorsk, wandering amid the wonderful churches and attending the service. He talked to me about architecture and icons. When I got home that evening, I sat on the couch with Mother and wept wildly. "What if he stops loving me?" Mama was surprised, but she understood. "He hasn't even fallen in love with you fully, and you're worried about his stopping."

Of course, he didn't stop right away, but fear and impatience poisoned our innocent love. He was always late, and every minute seemed an eternity. If he was pensive, I thought he was bored. If he hadn't kissed me yet, that meant I wasn't attractive. If he wanted to make love, that meant that this wasn't serious and he was just out for pleasure. And so on.

Now we are good friends, and our tormented affair is just a pleasant memory.

I met my future husband ten years later. I was different then. I had enough control not to rush him, not to impose my fears and worries on him. I think that I did my marriage campaign on a high level. But the question is, Was it worth it?

To be fully honest, I changed after the wedding. What happened to my patience and control? I thought that it was all his fault, that he was making me lose my temper. But what did he think? "Why has she changed? She used to be so gentle and understanding. And now it's hell." I can only guess what he thought. He usually said nothing.

SEPTEMBER 30. Yes, the reality of my family life clearly didn't correspond with my beautiful dreams. When we were in college, my girl friend and I would make a New Year's wish, write it on a piece of paper, burn it, and drink the ashes with a glass of champagne. The wish was always the same: "Meet *him*." An older friend used to joke coarsely, "What, are you waiting for a prince with blue balls?" And we were. We didn't want to get married because that meant the end of anticipation. We quoted the poet Marina Tsvetaeva: "Between the fullness of desire and the emptiness of execution my choice was made from the start." Love was something separate from real, everyday life. We read poetry: "I sent you a black rose in a goblet of wine gold as the sky." I was called "black rose" back in school. During class the boys would send me notes with a drawing of a black rose (was it interest, mockery, delight?).

My first kiss came at eighteen (retarded development?). An old Petersburg apartment (a love affair's not interesting in your own city; you need a journey with a meeting and separation), two in the morning, his parents asleep. Before the kiss we had tormented each other for several weeks, talking about life and death and reading poetry. And then, at last, I got up to go to the other room. He was in the doorway, our hands touched, and then I was in his arms. And there's the emptiness of execution: From a deity he turned into flesh and blood. The charms vanished, and all that was left were hands and lips. I didn't know how to kiss. He said that I had to open my mouth a bit and move my lips. We practiced for almost an hour, first between the door and the cupboard and then in the armchair. Afterward I couldn't fall asleep. The sweet mystery was turning into a still-not-understood reality. I decided that the first thing I had to do was learn how to kiss. I tried it on the pillow, but that didn't work. Instead of kissing, I was biting, and the pillow was all wet. I'd wait until morning. You obviously needed other lips.

There's no better city for being in love than St. Petersburg. The streets and squares double the intensity of your feelings. The angel atop the Alexander Column soars in the dark, scudding clouds, and the air is heavy and humid. I suppose that in sunny countries happiness has another flavor. There it is anxious, tormenting, and imbued with a cold fog.

A warm apartment, hot strong tea, lemon liqueur. Damned guests won't go away. I want to be alone with him. So that's what desire is: I'm hot; I'm feverish; I have a strange sensation in my belly. I don't understand what's happening to me. For me, desire is part of being in love. We don't even make an attempt to create anything. It's twilight, and we're lying under a blanket with our clothes on. All that exists for us is lips, hands, shoulders, my breasts. We don't touch the sweet, secret places.

We went to the beautiful suburbs around Petersburg, taking walks in the snowy paths of the palace grounds past marble statues that are boarded up. He said that you shouldn't kiss in the cold because your lips will crack. We kissed. On the way back we had a childish argument, and in the train he caressed and warmed my hands. He had received a college scholarship, and there was a farewell dinner in the luxurious Evropeiskaya Hotel. I couldn't taste the food; tears kept filling my eyes. What will happen to us?

Nothing. I went back to Moscow; his calls became rarer and rarer. Our next meeting took place a few months later, and it was sad and unnecessary. Then we saw each other rather frequently. We drank a bit and had a bit of fun and drove each other a bit crazy, but we didn't fall in love.

That was more than fifteen years ago. Now he's a professor, wise and talented, a bit odd, and profoundly religious. Incidentally, he never did marry.

OCTOBER 5. More about my husband. Gradually things came to an end. Sociologists have targeted the crisis years in a marriage. I think they're the second, fifth, and twentieth. Our crisis came in a year and a half. One fine morning I asked my husband to go back to his parents for a month. I had to force myself to do it; parting scared me, but our life together was impossible. He didn't argue; he packed and left. I wept the first night, and then it was wonderful. My friends and parents were proud of my determination and at the same time seemed to pity me. I was a sort of hero tricked by fate. I bought new clothes, started going out, and then . . . had an affair. I don't know whether I was finding myself or taking revenge. I loved the role of the disillusioned woman made wiser by experience and now betraying her husband at last. We made intellectual small talk until one o'clock (what if my husband were to come home?) and then . . . Around six I would chase out my seducer, to his great annoyance. My husband would appear when I was at work, leaving money and food.

After the month was up, it was his turn to take revenge. He said that he'd come back when he felt like it, maybe in another month. I was losing the initiative. I had to do something.

Here's a widespread Soviet story. A lousy husband, drunkard, hooligan, and womanizer perpetrates petty hooliganism, as it is called. Maybe he even beats up his wife. The police arrest him, and the next morning his wife, with a swollen, bruised face, runs to them and begs, "Give me back my bastard!" Of course, that's much too plebeian a version for me, but I had to get my "bastard" back anyway. Simply out of stubbornness. Ironically I offered him a chance to come back on March 8, International Women's Day. I was solidifying the international victory of women over men. I went to a friend's house—as if I weren't even waiting for him. He came home later than I did, returning into captivity with his head proudly held high.

OCTOBER 10. Now I can joke about it, but at the time it was sad and difficult to understand. We divorced eight months later.

You get married and divorced in the same building, the registry of civil documents. You go in for a divorce, and you're met by happy newlyweds on the way out. *I'd like to see you two years from now*, I thought spitefully.

You bring over the divorce documents and worry about going in the wrong room; you might get married by accident again. While we waited in line, my husband thought up a fun thing to do: get married and immediately go next door for a divorce. No one would care; you only have to wait three months.

When we registered our marriage (I hate that expression), everything was fun and silly: a woman with a red sash across her shoulder (the symbol of a solid Soviet family?), the memorized spiel, the band that isn't sick of playing the same wedding march every fifteen minutes. At the most solemn moment I got the giggles and couldn't hold it in. The woman must have thought that the not-very-young bride was suffocating with happiness. The groom couldn't understand what was expected from him when the woman suggested he congratulate me—i.e., kiss me. We obviously didn't belong at this Soviet ceremony.

The wedding certificate, a pretty piece of paper in a blue folder, looked decent. We checked that the names were right. Friends had had a curious thing happen. They got married, and at the wedding feast with relatives and friends, when an uncle jokingly proposed, "Let's look and see whom they married you to!" they looked at the certificate. The bride was correct, but the groom was a stranger. They were leaving on their honeymoon that evening, and they couldn't check into the hotel without proof of marriage. They hurried back, but the registry did only divorces in the afternoon. They had to make a scene in order to get a temporary certificate with the groom's name on it.

We didn't have a problem, and the registrar even spelled my husband's difficult name right. All I wanted to do was have a drink or even get drunk, and that is what I did. We went home, accepted the congratulations of the relatives and friends who had been waiting for us, and sat down to a luxurious feast. A half hour later I was tipsy, forgot about my new husband, and enjoyed our guests. By nightfall, when the honored relatives left and only the friends remained, I was dancing on the table.

The next day we left for our honeymoon in the Baltics— closer to civilization. My husband's relatives had given us a present: They arranged for us to stay at the Central Committee hotel. The closer to the Central Committee, the closer to Soviet rule and the farther from Europe, so there was no hot water, the bed collapsed after our first trial, and party fat cats were feeding in the restaurant downstairs. The hotel for foreigners across the street was a different matter: Finnish furniture, bars and restaurants, a sauna, and drunks—but at least they were Finns. At the Central Committee hotel the staff knew everyone and didn't ask for a passport or hotel pass or care about your family status. If party functionaries wanted to sin with other men's wives, that was their business and the party didn't interfere.

A strange alienation occurred in the early days of our honeymoon. Or was it just my imagination? We walked along the cozy streets of Tallinn, went to the best restaurants, drank beer, spent money, but I was sad.

Two years later we went next door in the registry building

to get our divorce. It was easy. If you don't want to divide up anything in court, you come back three months later, and you're as free as a bird. It only costs one hundred rubles. That's tidy income for the state since there are so many divorces. It's more complicated with property. There are no prenuptial agreements in the Soviet Union, so everything is divided in half. Your only hope is to prove that the furniture and so on were bought before the marriage. I know an intelligent young man who, after living for several years with his wife in her parents' apartment, tried to take away a blanket that they had purchased five years before the wedding. My neighbor took his own child's baby carriage during his divorce and gave it to the child of his future spouse. People have moral blackouts during divorce.

Our divorce was congenial. My husband took only the things from my apartment that were his. And he was not in a hurry to take them. The boxes in the corner were getting on my nerves. I wanted to get rid of the reminders quickly.

The first few months were hard. I lived alone in the apartment. There was no phone (my turn hadn't come up yet), and I wasn't ready for a new relationship. I felt sorry for myself, and I was enjoying my suffering. But I knew that I was still lovable and that men would travel to see me and bring me flowers and gifts.

OCTOBER 12. I often wonder why I got married. If I had it to do over again, what would I have done?

The same. It was a mistake that had to be made, like a

childhood disease, like measles or mumps or chicken pox. If you don't have it in time, a late case will be more severe. You have to build immunity.

Men seem to think that a marriage proposal is what women dream of most. Maybe, but not after an unhappy marriage.

I truly don't want to get married (for now?). I used to think that marriage was love and the expectation of evenings, wonderful nights, joyous holidays, and common interests. Now I know that it means heavy shopping bags, laundry, dishes, alienation, a weary face, and infrequent happy moments. The main thing is not to expect help from men and to do everything yourself—repairs around the house, the plumbing, earning money. I sometimes think that it would be good to have brothels for female clients. Then you're totally independent. I'm disgusted with myself even as I write this. I sound like an embittered Soviet feminist. What happened to the sweet romantic girl?

I probably took too long recovering from my "illness." I'm afraid to admit to myself that I'm a normal woman. I want a good husband, children, love, and that most hard-to-understand and elusive thing called happiness.

CHAPTER FOUR

Come, Guests, to My Party

OCTOBER 14. The phones never stop ringing in Moscow apartments. Everyone has his or her own "reception hours." Mine are from eleven in the morning until two in the morning. Even three, for European friends. We talk about everything from detergents at the neighborhood store to the fate of world civilization. You can talk twenty-four hours a day for two rubles and fifty kopecks a month. Of course, you pay more if you call another city.

The phone is right by my bed. I like to start the day with a phone call. I have friends with whom I talk weekly but haven't seen in years. There's something pathological about it since they're less than an hour away.

My grandparents in Kaluga had company almost every evening. They were poor, so they didn't serve anything special, but they always had tasty, strong tea. There was something of nobility and aristocracy about those visits. It would be dark and nasty outside, and a knock at the front door would bring in ladies wrapped in shawls, their escorts in galoshes over their shoes. The room was warm, and the lamp over the table in the big shade with fringe bathed the room in a soft yellow light. The guests headed straight for the stove to warm their hands. Then they sat down to play cards—a game called King. They never played for money since everyone had trouble making ends meet.

Then Grandmother went to the kitchen to make tea. Crackers, jam, and inexpensive candies were taken down from the enormous buffet. The hosts had their favorite cups, and the guests got the best china. Wine was not served.

I liked getting the sweets from the buffet. It was big, old, and mysterious. I thought it lived its own life; each shelf had its own smell. The doors creaked, and the bottom door kept falling off. To tell the truth, I used to hang on it and ride it back and forth. I was never punished for it, and Grandfather fixed it silently time after time.

The table conversation was always pleasant and soothing. The grown-ups didn't talk about politics; they were afraid, and there was really nothing to say in those years. They discussed city life and their friends. When there were other children visiting, Grandfather would play our favorite song on the piano. We held hands, moved in a circle, and sang:

> The cooks are making soup, soup, soup.
> A big spider in the kettle sits, sits, sits.

I don't know where that song came from.

We children used to take old clothes out of the trunk and play dress-up. We always had a big tree for New Year's. It took up half the room. We spent hours playing guessing games in front of it. One person picked a letter, and the rest tried to name a toy that began with it.

The town was a quiet one, and our guests didn't worry

about going home late, so they stayed. We would be put to bed, but we would hear voices from the living room.

We almost never went out. Everyone liked coming to our house. Papa told me that when he and his brother were little, it was even better. The family had the whole house. It was only later that as people used to say in the early days of Soviet rule, our family was compacted—that is, half the rooms were taken away for another family. Many guests came, and they played the piano and danced. Grandfather liked beautiful women (I guess that's why he married my grandma but didn't limit himself to her), and formerly chic ladies frequented our house. Once Papa ran into a room and found Grandfather kissing one. In the olden days famous musicians often came to the city, and they often visited our house and filled the rooms with music.

Funny incidents abounded. My grandparents had a pet white rat. Once, when the guests were leaving, one woman put on her fur coat and felt something in the sleeve. She screamed hysterically. The poor little animal, more frightened than the lady, ran across her back from one sleeve to the other, jumped out, and escaped. The lady was in a state for a long time. Then everyone laughed.

Usually the guests smoked a lot, filling the rooms with heavy clouds. The ladies kept up with the men. The little panes in the windows that could be opened in winter never were for some reason. No one thought that smoking was harmful then. Grandmother was very ill with emphysema later in life.

The realities of life in Kaluga are mixed up for me with the stories my grandparents and my father told me. Sometimes it all seems so far away that I can't believe I was ever there. I'd give so much to go back at least for a day. I often cry at night remembering those years.

OCTOBER 15. It's 2:00 A.M., and I'm not at all sleepy. Earlier I went out for five minutes and came back only now. And that's nothing. I have a Georgian friend who went out for a loaf of bread in Tbilisi and called his parents a few hours later from another part of the country—Leningrad. He had run into a friend who was going there, and they decided to fly together. Once a Moscow friend made a date with me, said he'd take a rest for a few hours, then would call me to pick me up. He vanished for three days: went to Tallinn to party with some friends. I sat by the phone worrying about all kinds of horrors—heart attack, mugging, kidnapping. He was a pig and should have called. But it's typical Moscow behavior; why bother with explanations?

Today a typically Moscow thing happened to me. I ran into friends of a friend who lives nearby. I had forgotten that they were having an opening at home—new paintings. That's part of Moscow's creative life—having exhibits at home or readings of new works. Luckily that's changing, and talented people are coming out from the underground (a phenomenon of the Brezhnev era). I went with them. Total freedom exists there: Wear what you want, bring whom you want (except sellouts), and do what you want. All different types of people were there—from Kazakhs to Americans. You couldn't tell who was who by just looking. Now-famous artists, with names in the West and bank accounts in Switzerland, are still wearing worn trousers and sweaters. Bohemians mauled by Soviet reality. I like being with them, even though I'm a bit of a stranger; I don't have their artistic insouciance and disdain for the stability of a bourgeois prosperity.

A lovely young Italian is a frequent visitor at this house. She has a marvelous job and wealthy businessmen boyfriends, but she runs off from all that to be with the Moscow bohemians. Her local boyfriends readily give themselves and their love and don't mind receiving Western presents and invitations to restaurants or even Paris in return. A slight contradiction from disdain for material values but, on the other hand, a forgivable weakness.

The food always varies, too—depending on what people bring. Lying next to dubious-looking Moscow sausage may be an exquisite French cheese, and a bottle of scotch next to a cheap wine from the neighborhood store. The conversation varies, too. No one tries to show off his or her erudition, though education is taken for granted.

Today was like every other day. We looked at paintings and slides and talked about them a bit. These discussions are like a small theatrical show—conditional and ironic. It's not an official arts council where the bureaucrats decide who can be an artist and who can't.

Then we "stretched" a bit. This is an expression that has become popular lately. It means having fun and relaxing. If you have a lot of fun, you have "stretched to your full height." Today wasn't to full height; it was moderate. By the way, people don't drink a lot here. They know how to have fun without that.

OCTOBER 17. I spent the evening at Mama's. Our old friends were there. It was all like before, but without the single and most important element. I just can't get used to the fact that Papa will never come into the room and make his usual jokes.

I lived my whole life with him, and he remains a mystery. I always thought that just a little bit more and he would reveal himself, I'd know everything about him. When I stood by his coffin in church, I looked at his face and tried to find an answer. He looked peaceful. There was even a shadow of his light, slightly ironic smile. The priest said to me, "Don't cry. Look at him; he left us in peace."

But he did not live with peace in his heart. And what person of his generation could live at peace with himself? Maybe Andrei Sakharov, with whom Papa had studied at the university. But only a few individuals could stand up to that monster system that broke the wisest, most honest and talented people. Papa was helpless in the face of intrigue, lies, and hypocrisy. He would retreat. And his family paid for it. He'd bring home the stress of the day's foolishness and humiliations. It was all so simple: He was a scientist, and all he needed and wanted was to do his work until he was exhausted and sleepless. He didn't fear that. He could work twenty hours a day until he collapsed with fatigue. By the way, he never had a study at home. We were always crowded first in one room and then in two. It was only after I married and left home that he had a room to himself where he could work and sleep.

At home I remember him mostly lying on the couch reading. That was his usual state. His knowledge was astonishing and unexpected. He could name all the German and American generals of World War II, lead us across the main bridges of

Venice (without ever having been there), and name all the states of the United States. He knew all the draft versions of *War and Peace* and could find any spot in his beloved book in a flash. My German friends, after having spent their first evening with my father at our home, couldn't believe that he lived in a tiny apartment and didn't head a big department at a leading university. In three hours in perfect German he told them more about Europe than they, having spent their lives there, knew.

I got a significant part of my education at home, at the family table. Often over lunch or dinner in the kitchen, we discussed history and literature for hours, debating and sometimes even arguing. Mama was a good cook, but the best treat when we had guests was table conversation. After eating, we drank tea endlessly, sometimes until two in the morning, without running out of things to talk about. You could say anything at all, except stupid things. Father grew annoyed if Mama or I made a stupid comment (he didn't pick on the guests). He taught me to think and to phrase my thoughts precisely. As I write this diary, I think that he'd let me have it over a lot that's in here.

OCTOBER 19. Today is one of those horrible days when you don't want to see anyone or talk to anyone.

Many years ago, when I worked with Americans, a charming old man asked, "Tell me, is it true that you have no toilet paper and that your women eat their children?" I said that the first was absolutely true, and the second clearly exaggerated. A sweet woman asked me, "Do Soviet women menstruate?" Of course, the questions weren't the brightest, but it's our own fault. We created an image of ourselves as savages. In the seventies such fine specimens of *Homo sovieticus* went abroad that people could easily suppose that we were from another planet.

Yes, we menstruate, and we have PMS, too. You can't explain that condition to men. Everything is a dirty gray with black veins. You grab hold of every gloomy thought and develop it. Today I'm feeling global depression over my lost life. I'll be forty in a few years, and what have I achieved? I'm divorced, I have no children, I'm alone, and no one needs me. I've studied all my life, and I know so little. I don't feel like going to work. I'm sick of it here. The weather's bad; I can't even go for a walk. I shut the curtains, got back in bed, and enjoyed my misery.

Then the phone rang; it was a girl friend. She has her own problems. She's pregnant. She doesn't want to have this second child. She can't handle it. Her husband has a small salary, and her job is important for the family. The first child is a burden on her own mother. She doesn't want to have the baby, but she's afraid to go to the hospital. She's looking for a doctor recommended by friends because it's scary to have an abortion in the general crowd. Besides, this isn't her first time, and she always has complications. I forgot my mood; after all, PMS is better than an unwanted pregnancy.

I hung up and called a former boyfriend, a doctor. I think I'm lucky. He has a gynecologist friend, and he'll call him and set things up. It's an excuse for us to meet. He'll bring his friend, wine, and snacks, and we'll go see my miserable friend. Her husband is on a business trip. She hasn't told him anything. He wants a child.

In Moscow many medical and work issues are discussed at

the table. I once saw the following. I went to see doctor friends who were having a party. Two mafiosi types were at their table, drinking heavily. One of them had an implanted ampoule that makes you unable to tolerate alcohol. It's the way we treat alcoholism. He was sick of it and wanted to start drinking again but was afraid of the reaction. He brought a bottle of cognac and his best friend to drink under a doctor's supervision. The evening went well. He drank a lot and with pleasure without any obvious effect on his health. Apparently his organism had adjusted to the ampoule.

Well, back to my miserable day. I think my mood has improved. The best medicine is someone else's trouble. That's the lousy way we are, much as I hate to admit it. My friend's problems brought me out of my depression. I took a shower, dressed, and went to see friends.

OCTOBER 21. My doctor friend didn't call yesterday or the day before, the usual Moscow story. My friend Katya dropped by. We were both in a lousy mood, and we were sitting in the kitchen having tea and feeling sorry for ourselves. We wanted to go out and have fun, but where? My lost friend finally called and said he was on his way with the gynecologist. Not a great amusement, but better than being alone and cranky. Plus my pregnant friend was waiting.

They're both married and middle-aged men. It's silly to generalize, but our men are all alike. They never miss a chance to have fun on the side. They consider it a small diversion from the grayness of daily life. They may be right, for our life is awfully monotonous and joyless. You can't take your wife out to a restaurant. You can't get in on Friday or Saturday night, and if you do by some miracle, you will get a load of negative experiences. The food will be cold, the champagne warm, and the waiter will be rude and cheat you. Besides, you have to drink. If you go out in the evening and don't order at least two hundred grams of cognac, a bottle of vodka, a bottle of wine, five or six types of zakuski, a main course, ice cream, and coffee, the waiter will despise you. So just for the two of you, you have to spend half your monthly salary.

Isn't it better to visit an unmarried woman? You bring a bottle of wine, a crummy bouquet, and you're given food, drink, and maybe even . . . Moscow men are not generous. A young friend of mine told me, "Mama told me that if I go to see a woman, she must give me food and drink and some to take home." Of course, his mother was just the opposite. She took men for a bundle.

Maybe it's our own fault. We women take it all without a whimper. We always have food in the refrigerator and a bottle of wine—just come.

I hate writing about this. Where did this psychology come from? I think it starts at school. Once I dropped by to see friends of my parents, a wonderful intellectual family. Their erudite son was home alone and bored. Suddenly he got an idea: He called his female classmates and invited them over. His condition was to bring wine, preferably more than one bottle. Fifteen minutes later there was a horde of girls with bottles and food, and a few minutes later, miraculously, a crowd of boys ready to drink appeared. They turned on the music, drank and danced and kissed on the balcony. About two hours later our host got bored. He opened the door and chased everyone out except two pals and me (I was from a different category). I remember it very well. He stood at the wide open door and pushed people out. He even used a mop to make his point.

Mama never believed me. She thought I exaggerated. Recently she saw for herself. It was one of our many revolutionary holidays, and I was at home, as usual. This time I was in an old sweat suit spattered with paint, redecorating the kitchen. A friend telephoned. An educated, well-to-do young man, he had been at a party and been drinking. He was in a good mood, and he wanted to see me. My mother's presence and my protests didn't stop him. He came by taxi and called again from downstairs. I couldn't chase him away. He came up, ate, drank some more, and told me about his trip to Switzerland. Then he began to feel the partying: He had a headache and wanted to sleep. Kindhearted Mama suggested he take a nap. But he had completed his program, and now he wanted to go home. I went out into the hall to say good-bye, and he started rummaging in his bag. Well, I thought, a souvenir from Switzerland. No way! He was looking for money. He didn't have enough for a cab. I had to lend him five. When I got back to the kitchen, my naïve mother asked what he had brought me from Switzerland. We both still have illusions. When I told her about the five rubles, she burst out laughing. Laughter through tears. What can you expect when the richest men come to your birthday with bottles that they drink themselves?

The doctors were generous; they brought food and drink. The food wasn't anything fancy—a can of peas, some canned fish, and a dozen eggs. It wasn't a very refined meal, but there was a lot of good cognac. We decided to eat first and then go to Anya's. Katya and I drank a lot to cheer up. The conversation didn't go well, but the cognac helped. We remembered Anya and went to her place. As usual, she immediately set the table and brought out the wine, and we had more to eat and drink. Then we discussed her medical problem.

We spent the night at Anya's. No, there was no sex; no one needed anyone else. What a stupid evening!

OCTOBER 24. Most of all, I like visiting our family friend Luba and her mother. It's like going to another century. They have a small apartment in a building of the Stalin era. The house is surrounded by ugly factories and chimneys. The courtyard and entryway are filthy and smelly. But when you shut the door, you enter old Moscow. The old mismatched furniture, placed to create warmth and coziness, evokes a special atmosphere. Photographs of grandfathers and great-grandfathers speak of their noble heritage. Theirs is a mixed line: Italian, German, French, Russian, Armenian. I can never take my eyes from the picture of Luba's grandfather: high forehead and a noble and slightly haughty profile. He was shot in the twenties, when he was only twenty-seven. Her other grandfather, the Armenian, came to the Soviet Union from Persia in the thirties. He had been a Communist there and became an "enemy of the people" here. He spent several years in prison and survived miraculously. Luba's mother went to Moscow to see Stalin's chief executioner, to beg for her father's life. The incredible happened: He was released from prison. That was one of the mysteries of the Stalin era: Some people were spared unexpectedly. Luba's grandfather returned taciturn and never spoke about prison. When his daughter washed him, it pained her to see the horrible scars on his back. Her father shopped only at the free markets. He didn't want to have any contact with the Soviet regime, even in the stores.

I always find spiritual peace in this home. People live by eternal values here. Luba is devout and goes to church. She is beautiful but disregards it, dressing modestly and a bit old-fashionedly. Her mother was very lovely in her youth. There is a portrait of her done by a famous Armenian artist. She used to paint, and some of her exquisite watercolors hang over the big couch. There is also a small Persian rug, hand-knotted, which is said to be very valuable. Plates with portraits of the imperial family hang on the walls, part of a large service now lost.

The food is always delicious. There are some specialties of the house. The table is set beautifully, and dinner turns into a ritual, just like the olden days. We almost never drink. It's not necessary here. I once said that people should be brought here as if for treatment; all your anxieties and fears go away.

Both women are contemporary and follow current events. Luba lives a life that is a strange mix of the bohemian and the religious. She has never married, but it would be hard to find the right candidate for this house.

She and her mother are always helping someone, and there are always friends or relatives staying with them, sometimes shamefully abusing the hospitality.

When I feel down, I call Luba's mother. I go over, we have tea in the kitchen and talk, and things fall into place for me. The wisdom and spiritual nobility of this woman are astonishing. Age has not diminished her attraction or charm. She is always well dressed. She wears lovely old rings on her fingers and gorgeous beads on her neck.

And she makes the best tea in Moscow, the best pies, and the best jam.

Their apartment was always an attraction for our entire family. Father, who didn't like going out, was prepared to spend endless evenings here. Even my not very convivial husband told his secrets to Luba's mother.

Every time I leave their home, I think, *God grant them health and strength.*

OCTOBER 27. The eternal and rather naïve question: Why is there so much evil in the world? Like a chain reaction, it gives birth to more evil and grows to gigantic proportions. You could write a science-fiction story about a city choking on evil. Usually the meanest and least attractive places are big cities. Muscovites, for instance, have the reputation for being grim and rude.

I believe that an energy aura, one of dirty brown or light gold, hovers over a city much as it does over a person. Moscow is a heavy city. When you come back from vacation, even before you get tired from work, you can feel your good energy dying. The rested look is vanquished: Faces are drawn; there are bags under the eyes. Many of my friends have noticed it, too.

People can't deal with the constant hassles that wear them out more than big problems. The irritation grows. They take it out on someone else, and it goes on. . . . Some are so used to it that they've forgotten about any other mood. Many years ago I was traveling in Greece with a group of Soviet tourists. I got into the bus one morning and everyone was very gloomy. I said, "Look, it's a sunny day, we're about to travel around a marvelous country, why don't you smile?" The answer was: "We paid our money; we can smile or not as we want." A fine answer!

In Moscow you're regarded as an enemy when you enter any office or place of business. In the stores you're hated by the clerks and cashiers, in the toilets by the cleaning women, at the hospitals by the doctors and nurses. They forget that once they leave work, they'll be treated the same way. In the morning in crowded buses and the metro people push you angrily for no reason. I often catch myself wanting to hit someone just to release my tension. A friend once told me, "Just pick someone out on the street, run over, hit him hard, and run away. You'll feel so good afterward."

Maybe that's why we like going to see friends, in search of those islands of goodness. I often hum Okudjava's "Georgian Song" to myself: "I'll plant a grape seed in the warm soil, and I'll kiss the vine and pick the ripe grapes. And I'll call my friends and tune my heart to love, otherwise what am I living for on this earth?" When will we all tune our hearts to love?

OCTOBER 29. This is a very strange "intimate" diary. A normal woman should write about affairs, torments of love, stormy nights of passion. There's a joke about it. The teachers say, "Today we will be talking about love. No, no, not love for parents, everyone knows that. And don't look at me with those shiny eyes. No, we're not going to talk about love between men and women. That's not the most important thing in life. Today we are going to talk about love . . . for the Communist party, the most beautiful, lofty, and pure love."

No matter how we resisted, they forced that absurd psychology on us drop by drop like poison. And really, if human life isn't worth anything, then what can you expect of personal life?

By the way, women of the early revolutionary years weren't very consistent. Preaching total loyalty to Communist ideas, they also threw themselves into many affairs. They thought it was a step toward the emancipation of women.

So I have nothing to write about love today. All the men are busy with more important things; no one is calling. But I want so much to get dressed up, set the table with candles, put the roses he brings into a vase, and spend a lovely evening together.

OCTOBER 30. I love to cook. It is a form of creativity for me. Luckily, living alone, I can cook when inspiration moves me and not because I must. A lavish and delicious table is one of the mysteries of Soviet life. The stores are empty, but the tables are full. Russian tradition calls for various zakuski, or hors d'oeuvres, then the main course, and then dessert, usually a homemade cake.

I keep the house stocked with delicious canned goods, ham and sausage from Germany, and chocolates. When you expect guests for a birthday or some other big occasion, you start preparing weeks in advance. You go to the store regularly. One time out of five you'll be in luck; you buy something that is a usually unavailable item. Then you put your haul together and see what you can make out of it. The process is always creative because you never have all you need and you have to figure out what to substitute. Either you come up with unexpected dishes or you throw everything out (I don't do that).

Cooking is an adventure. You never know whether the meat will be tender or tough, whether the chicken will taste of chicken or the fish it was fed.

You start cooking two days before the party. The first day you wash everything and get it ready since you bring stuff home from the stores in very unsanitary condition. The meat is on a big bone; the chicken still has a few pinfeathers; the vegetables are covered with dirt. The stores tried selling washed carrots and potatoes recently, but the vegetables rotted from being wet before they were bought. It's better to wash them at home. You actually cook the next day. Sometimes you get so tired that by the time the guests arrive you're ready for bed. Some creativity!

I try to streamline the process: I make lists, do things in consecutive order, and get my mother to help. The results are worth it. I sit at the table and wearily watch the guests enjoy the numerous salads, the herring in different sauces, the meat or chicken, and slices of cake. And I'm in a good mood because I've had a few drinks and have forgotten the long road to success.

NOVEMBER 2. Today I made friends with our valiant Soviet police. Some Moscow friends brought over their Polish friends who work here. They all are older, from a more vivacious generation that has not lost its lust for life. A bottle of the famous

Wyborowa vodka appeared on the table. Every time it was empty, Jan ran down to the car for another one. A joking ritual. I don't remember how many times he went downstairs, but it was a lot.

That reminds me of an American who visited a Georgian writer. The table groaned with food, but there was just one bottle of wine. The guests couldn't understand why. They sat down. The host poured the wine and knocked on the door near the table. It opened, and a hand reached out. It took the empty bottle and returned it refilled a moment later. The wine pourer did his work well. The bottle vanished and reappeared several dozen times.

So our bottle simply appeared. Of course, we had a good time, with dancing and noise. A neighbor dropped by with her friend. And suddenly there was a horrible banging on the pipes—my downstairs neighbor. She is as invincible as Soviet power. She is always fighting for "justice." At the co-op meetings she stands up for the rights of the working class and tries to get her few kopecks from the corrupt co-op board. I feel sorry for her. She had a hard life, but she's too full of communal squabbling. She could have put up with one evening. I have noisy guests once in a hundred years.

It got late. The guests left, except for the neighbor. Suddenly the bell rang, and there were two policemen at the door. I invited them in. "Look, it's quiet, we had a birthday party, we had a little fun." (You have to lie a little.) It was cold and dark outside, so I invited them (their names were Petya and Lyosha) to get warm and have a bite to eat. We drank, too, and the police enjoyed their snack. They gave me some advice as they left: If the downstairs neighbor tries to ruin another party, call an ambulance to come get her. They also offered to help me when I needed to buy vodka. During the day they maintain order at the line in the liquor store, and they'll let me get to the head of the line.

Now I believe that my police force takes care of me!

NOVEMBER 5. The educated Russian (and I dare consider myself one) knows the value of the Russian language and does not want to damage it. We all are scribblers in our souls but don't dare reveal this innocent but dangerous sin.

A diary is a compromise. You seem to be writing only for yourself, but with a secret hope that maybe . . . It's hard to judge your own work. Today it doesn't seem bad, not at all, and tomorrow you want to burn the whole thing.

I've read what I've written to try to see if I've got the makings of a writer. I'll read a few excerpts to friends and see what they have to say.

NOVEMBER 8. Here's what happened.

One wise and honest friend said, "It's boring and a little draggy. Your childhood reminiscences are important for you, but will anyone else care?" And really, writing about a Russian childhood after Bunin and Nabokov . . .

Another said that I wasn't frank enough. "Write with your guts, not your head." I don't have strength in my guts. I'm both patient and analyst here. If I just turn myself inside out and don't look at it dispassionately, I won't be far from going mad. After all, it's only my rationalism that has saved me living in this country.

But my girl friend liked it. She said I had talent but not enough mastery yet.

I console myself; even famous writers had mediocre first books. I'll practice on this diary. If it falls into someone's hands, that's his business.

NOVEMBER 9. They say that when a society is falling apart, mysticism thrives. Moscow is infected with it. Everyone is seeking miracles. Thousands sit by the TV and listen to the hypnotic speeches of Dr. Kashpirovsky. "Everything is fine, good, good. Your problems and pains are leaving; you feel lighter and more radiant." He is an honest man. "Some people may feel worse, but do not despair." After one of his shows a famous Moscow liberal said during a political talk, "Let's see, maybe some people really will feel better and some will be worse off. However, I doubt that anyone could be worse; we're at bottom now."

There was a funny parody on Radio Liberty. "Calm down, relax, dear comrades. Soviet power is gone, gone, gone. . . ."

In the early eighties, such a difficult period, I spent a lot of leisure time with my parapsychologist friends. They had an answer for everything: how to charm a man; how to overcome disease; how to withstand the dark forces around us. They really did try to help. Despite the semiofficial ban, they regularly went to their lab, an ancient, dilapidated building in the middle of Moscow. Patients in despair came there, and some were helped by the kind healers. The parapsychologists themselves were often strange and miserable.

It was white magic against the background of the black magic that traveled around Moscow in black Volgas and stuffed itself with black caviar. I realized that a devout person should not go near even white magic. Maybe my faith wasn't strong enough. However, I saw devout Christians there, too.

We often met at home. Famous scientists, doctors, and actors came. There was something Masonic about it. No, no, no, not a "kike-Masonic conspiracy" against the Russians. Actually there often were mysterious Asians at these evenings.

On holidays we succumbed to very earthly fun with lots of food and wine. But strangely we drank quite a bit and didn't get drunk. There was a special energy at the table. It could change the taste of vodka, so instead of being disgustingly bitter, it was almost sweet. What was that, hypnosis?

Women's charms were appreciated then. The men yielded to the magic power of the female force. Sometimes funny things happened. One highly respected doctor fell in love with me in the middle of the party (the influence of the sweet vodka?). He sat down next to me and started making passes. His wife didn't like it, of course, and she went home. The doctor was sent home after her. He reached his apartment and then suddenly ran back downstairs. He sat down on the steps and said, "No, I'm not going back to that bitch." It took his not very sober friend a lot of effort to bring him to "that bitch." Luckily everyone was in a good mood, and no one was angry or hurt.

My friend asked me, "Why are you wasting time on that mystical nonsense? Why don't you get real?" Actually it opened up a new dimension in my life. I learned the basics of Eastern religions and learned to control myself better and to understand others. When I went to India a few years later, I could see the power and spiritual beauty of that marvelous land beyond the poverty and filth. Besides, I was prepared for a mysterious revelation on the island of Crete, where fate brought me by accident. I'll write about it sometime.

NOVEMBER 10. The past pursues me. A crazy thought: Sometimes I want to die in order to return to the past. Is it weakness, helplessness in the face of real life? Everything that is bad or sad in the past now seems magical to me. I think that if I made just a small effort, I could return to those scents, sounds, and feelings. Suddenly everything comes at once: the smells of the old buffet in our Kaluga apartment; the aromatic tobacco plants in the city park; the sound of the old clock in our living room; the creak of the front door; the crackle of logs in the stove. If we do exist after death, maybe we can look back into the past from the other world? Can my father see me not just at this moment but also in my childhood? I think I believe that he can. It would be good if you could combine things from the past the way you wanted, say, invite all the people who are dear and interesting to you, even if they have lived at various times. What if you had the opportunity to invite twenty people now gone. Anyone at all—children, parents, Alexander the Great, Pushkin, Mozart. "Come, ghosts, to my party." I wonder if anyone will invite me when I die.

CHAPTER FIVE

Who Are the Real Feminists?

NOVEMBER 11. My best friend, Lena, married an American. She's not a friend anymore because she has stopped seeing everyone, including me. She's leaving for New York in a few days. I wonder if she'll call to say good-bye. Of course, it hurts that she's behaving this way. We have many years of real friendship behind us. But she was always a complicated person, and now, apparently, she is confused by her own emotions. Lena often went to extremes—she grieved to despair and loved to the exclusion of the rest of the world—and she understands that her friends may be envious that she's going to the land so many dream of and can't have, America.

NOVEMBER 12. "We'll do fine without America," my friend Dasha says. It's easy for her, she's almost always in love. Each time he's the best, most talented, and most beloved, and the next one is even better and even smarter. If men could change in accordance with her opinions, there would be no limit to their perfection.

Dasha is a sweetie—gentle, feminine, and charming. Men melt in her presence; she enchants them. Maybe it's a good thing that she's not going to America. She'd drive the poor men crazy there.

She has so much energy. She can party all night, go to work the next day, and go to another party that night. Sometimes I feel like an old wreck next to her.

We were in the kitchen having tea, and she was telling me about her new lover. He is an artist, a genius, of course. She met him at someone's house a few days ago, and the affair is just starting. He is having a big show, and she rushes over after work to help set up. I imagine that she won't be reachable for the next few days. They'll be devoted to him alone. I ask her at least to phone and let me know how things are going.

NOVEMBER 14. Dasha called and told me a fabulous story. Her more or less steady boyfriend was on a business trip. She invited the artist to her house. Everything was ready for her new love, the bell rang, and . . . there was her steady, Viktor, who was supposed to be in another city. He was all smiles, happy to have surprised her. She was in shock. The bell would ring again, Viktor would answer, and she'd be lost.

She began kissing Viktor and pulling him toward the bedroom. He wanted to take a shower, having just returned from a long trip. "Later, later," Dasha whispered passionately. "I missed you so much." They were in bed, the lights were out, and the doorbell rang, but no one would answer! "I'm sick of that neighbor," Dasha said. The artist saw that there was no light, and she planned to tell him that she had had to leave on an emergency.

Men, if this diary should fall into your hands, do not read the next lines. The next day Viktor told that "persistent neighbor," "You can't imagine how much Dasha loves me. She was trembling with passion when I showed up unexpectedly. She pulled me into bed, wouldn't even let me shower first."

NOVEMBER 15. I don't know about my friend Lena, but we can't handle competition with American women.

Today I watched two parts of an American soap opera on video. Are they trying to fool us naïve Soviet women, or is it true? The women are perfectly dressed; they look good at every age; they suffer beautifully; their tears fall without messing up their mascara. All their emotions are on their face, and they don't run around the room or break dishes. You think, *What willpower. Her life is falling apart, but her hair is done, her makeup is in place, and she's wearing extravagant jewelry. American men are so lucky; even in suffering their women are lovely. No wonder that men still love their wives after they leave them.* I know this is the movies (I tell myself slowly and dreamily), but I'm still envious.

I'm sure I wasn't very attractive during arguments with my husband: eyes swollen with tears, a red nose, dripping mascara smears, and an angry or miserable face (depending on the topic). Our fights were not pretty. I have to practice for the future; I'll have to go to the bathroom from time to time to powder my nose or put on lipstick. Maybe the arguments will be different, too?

And that marvelous immobility of the face—all the emotions are in the eyes. Our women move all the parts of their face during a fight. It releases the tension better.

So, girls, watch American movies, and study, study, study. It's hard, I know. After an argument their women sit on a pretty sofa in a marvelously appointed room and have a glass of wine (smoking is out of style), or they fly off to Paris to forget or go out to lunch with a girl friend. There are lots of variations. Our woman, licking tears from her lips, goes to the bathroom to finish the laundry or to the kitchen to make dinner or maybe to the store to stand in line for a while.

But who has it easier when it comes to getting over an argument? My unexpected conclusion is our woman. The other continues to suffer in her Mercedes, in her airplane, or at the lunch table. Ours forgets about it in a few minutes—because she has to continue her great struggle for survival. And if she manages to buy a deficit product or if she finds French cosmetics at the store, she is a victor.

As Gogol said, "Whom are you laughing at? You are laughing at yourselves."

NOVEMBER 18. Which of my friends is the happiest? Which can be envied with good jealousy? I think the lucky ones are those who live for today, go out, and have a good time. In order to do that, you have to be either very silly or very strong. Dasha is frivolous. She can cast away her worries, even though she gets depressed now and then. Another friend, Nina, is independent and self-confident. She always has a lot of money; she dresses well and rides around in her own car (that's a luxury for a woman in Moscow). She has a lot of men, but she knows that she can depend only on herself. She allows men to court her handsomely and expensively, but she keeps a distance: Men have to be kept in constant tension. However, that's easy to do when you're good-looking, and she is. She has big hazel eyes, a refined nose, beautiful, sensuous lips, light hair, and a terrific figure. All this is multiplied by inexhaustible energy, charm, and pure feminine self-confidence. We are walking down a hallway in a restaurant. She is tipsy and in a good mood. "Make way, I'm coming," she tells the men standing in our way. Delighted smiles follow her.

But her female wisdom came the hard way. Her husband cheated on her; she had a nervous breakdown and a few years of loneliness. Now it's all part of another life for her.

She is what is called a woman to the marrow of her bones. You can't learn it; you have to be born with it. A woman like that can drive men crazy to the end of her days. Nina even manages the horrors of our life easily. She is living proof that a woman can survive with fewer losses than a man in our Soviet conditions.

NOVEMBER 20. So Lena left for New York today without calling. Fifteen years of friendship thrown away so lightly! Many years ago, when we were younger, an adult friend said, "Just watch, your great friendship will last only until one of you falls in love seriously." She was right.

My practical friend Katya said, "You should have swallowed your pride and gone to Lena and asked her to send some men from America. Ugly ones, they're easier to catch." Katya is younger than I am but has been married three times. After her last divorce she announced, "I've had it with Russian men; the next time I'm marrying a foreigner." Katya is a pretty and seemingly gentle young woman with an iron grip. She doesn't like to work, but she likes to dress well, wear expensive jewelry, go to expensive restaurants, and drink champagne. I suppose she really should find an American. People say American men don't refuse their wives anything. The trick is to catch a rich one, and then you can do whatever you want with him. I don't believe these stories too much. But Katya may actually succeed; she's a determined woman. Her former husbands will remember her for life. She threw a plate of food at the first one, cut his brow, and he had to get stitches. She broke the second one's tooth. I don't know either man. Maybe they deserved it. I like Katya's sincerity when she explains the tactics of dealing with men: "You have to catch him on payday and take all his money."

"What is he supposed to live on?" I ask naïvely.

"That's his problem."

Her aggressiveness is hidden by her helplessness. What man can refuse a weak woman?

It's probably not nice writing this way about a friend, but she's more an acquaintance than a real friend. Besides, she tries her tricks on us, too, not just men, and that's not honest. If we're united against men, we have to keep our ranks tight. However, there's much that can be learned from Katya. But why is the result always so pitiful?

NOVEMBER 22. Today is the anniversary of John F. Kennedy's death. I came home from school many years ago, and my mother told me that he had been killed. I remember that I stood in the hall by the map and wept. He was an idol for us, the embodiment of the beautiful American dream. We were interested in every detail of his life. We read his speeches; we knew some of his words by heart. We were thrilled by his behavior during the Cuban crisis, even though we were on the other side. And he was also simply an attractive man, and we were all a little bit in love with him. His life with Jacqueline seemed like a model for family life, and she was our ideal. We tried to get copies of *America* magazine and spent hours poring over pictures of them and discussing her clothes, her hair, her poses. My friends were as crazy about her as about a movie star.

After the President's death many books were eventually published about him in the Soviet Union. I think we remembered and revered him more than people did in America.

A few years ago I got an American book about him and his wife. I couldn't believe it. It seems he cheated on his wife, was a bad husband, and often behaved egoistically and cruelly. I really don't want to believe that. It's hard to give up your childhood idols.

NOVEMBER 24. I can see that Western women who defend their rights are not going to like this, but they probably don't know the destructive power of those rights. Almost all my girl friends work. They have pretty good careers, but I don't know one who complains about inequality. Our desperate plea is

"Take away half our rights and let us simply be women." Let's look at the word "feminist." *Femina* means "woman," so the struggle is for the right to be a woman, not a man. Then who are the real feminists, they or we?

I think that many of my friends dream of finding a foreign husband so that they can escape to the world of "inequality." We're tired of being everything—wife, mother, housewife, financial support, boss, and subordinate. We want to be weak and helpless. We want to give ourselves up into slavery. But no one will take us. *Our* slaveholders are too weak.

Women like Nina are rare. Her strength is in her femininity. You have to be born with it and be able to preserve it. That's an almost impossible task in our society.

NOVEMBER 28. I got hold of an American book, *The Joy of Sex*. Everything is described very well and in great detail, with marvelous illustrations. You can read and learn. Until just recently sex was a banned topic. Children learned the basics of sex in school hallways and, at best, from their parents, who warned them against it. The main question was: Are you having sex or not? No one discussed how to have it. All forms of sexual contact, besides the most traditional, were considered deeply perverted and were discussed only in whispers. I remember Mama telling a friend about an affair a mutual friend was having: "And then he tried to get her to do a perversion, and she refused, naturally."

"What's a perversion?" I asked. It turned out she meant oral sex, for which we don't even have a proper word in Russian.

We always considered pregnancy the inevitable punishment for sex. All the warnings adults gave us were that you'd get pregnant and you'd have to have an abortion and it would hurt. In addition, no one would want to marry you later. You could also catch some vile disease, and that would shame you for life.

No joy was supposed to be connected with sex. I guess we talked about sex more in college, when sex was a theory, not a practice. As adults we readily discussed the consequences—that is, unwanted pregnancies. I never knew if my friends were ever satisfied, if their husbands and lovers were skillful and enlightened.

Now times are changing. There are erotic scenes on television and discussions of sexual problems, and women are no longer ashamed of their desires. Now every movie has to have a sex scene to be considered a movie. I suppose it's time for my friends to get together and share our experiences. We might learn a lot.

NOVEMBER 30.   I wonder where Lena is. Could she be walking around New York, enjoying American life? I envy her being in such an unusual city, although Americans have different opinions of it. "It's the center of the world, the city with everything," some say. "Disgusting, scary city, it's not American at all," others have told me. Lena will see for herself, but I doubt she'll tell me about it. I don't think I'll ever see her again.

Today Anya and I confirmed that Moscow can't compete with New York. Her family's away, she's free, and we decided to go out to eat. I put on high-heeled boots, a black hat, a lovely

Swiss coat, and we met in the metro and rode into town. We went to almost all the restaurants on Gorky Street. Some were full; others were closed for the mysterious "special service." It's never clear who is getting special service. My feet were beginning to hurt, and I was very hungry. We got back in the metro and went to the Praga, one of the biggest restaurants in Moscow. There wasn't a table in any of its many rooms. We sadly wandered down the street and heard music coming from the Doctor's Club. "Maybe we'll be in luck here," we said, holding our breaths. Alas, the young men at the door said, "Today is an evening for internationalist Komsomol members."

"We'd like to go to the snack bar," we said meekly.

"The snack bar is only for Komsomol members tonight."

By then all I wanted was to go home, take off my boots, get into my robe, eat in my kitchen, where there is a free table and you don't have to be a Komsomol to be fed, and then go to bed. But on the way home Anya persuaded me to go to her place. We took out a bottle of wine, heated up a fine dinner, and gradually forgot about our misadventures. I came home happy and relaxed. "Where did you go, which restaurant?" Mama asked on the phone.

"The best—Anya's kitchen."

DECEMBER 1. I don't know what the hell's the matter with me, I'm swearing right and left. I have an almost scientific theory about it. People swear for two reasons: a limited vocabulary or an excess of emotion, usually negative. Of course, I put myself in the latter category. Russian swearing is unique. It's not your twenty or thirty English curses. We can combine over two hundred words to create the so-called big circle. There's also a small one, which uses around seventy words, if I'm not mistaken. At Moscow University this story circulated. A pretty and frail woman was walking through the university courtyard. She heard horrible swearing coming from a manhole where workmen were fixing the pipes. She bent over and told them that they weren't swearing properly. She ended up sitting on the ground, her elegant legs dangling in the manhole, lecturing the workmen on Russian cursewords. They didn't know that the lady was a famous philologist, a Ph.D., whose dissertation had been on that very expressive part of Russian. Russian village women have the most expressive vocabularies. A friend once heard a peasant woman talking to a rooster in her hen house. It was an incomparable monologue, juicy and funny.

There are a lot of jokes in Moscow about weakling intellectuals using swearwords. A meek intellectual in glasses and hat is riding in a crowded bus. His huge neighbor keeps stepping on his foot. The intellectual keeps asking, "Comrade, please move your foot." The reply is always "Fuck off." At last the egghead gets really mad and counters with "On principle I refuse to fuck off."

My girl friends curse a lot, too, but there is a taboo: not in front of men. Men restrain themselves in front of us, too.

I'm certain that it's impossible to live in our times without swearing. You'd choke on suppressed emotions. Say you come to work and learn that you're scheduled to lecture on Saturday, when you've made weekend plans. "Shit!" you say inadvertently. Or you're watching a session of the Supreme Soviet on TV. A dyed-in-the-wool conservative is defending the unshakable foundations of socialism. "Asshole, look around, see what's happening to the country," you say. The audience applauds wildly. "Go fuck yourselves" is the only reply to make as you turn off the set.

DECEMBER 3. I watched a sad and rather disgusting scene today. I was visiting friends. The head of the house is a writer, almost a dissident. We were having tea in the kitchen when a friend came over with her new date. She looked awful and was stinking drunk. Her companion was strange and suspicious-looking. He said he was with the circus. Where does she dig them up? These attempts at happiness won't lead to anything good. She's divorced and lives with her school-age son in the same apartment as her ex-husband; they can't trade their small two-room apartment for two apartments. Of course, she wants to remarry and have a normal life, but where can she find a decent man at her age? They all have families, too.

She got sick and went to the bathroom to throw up. The circus guy kept chattering about something. The writer suddenly blew up. He felt bad for Tanya and decided to throw out her date, who stood in the corridor and refused to leave. I thought there would be a fight. We stayed in the kitchen, keeping quiet. After fifteen minutes the door slammed. Tanya, pale, came out of the bathroom. We gave her some strong tea. The furious writer came back in. "You bitch, why do you bring people like that into my house? I have enough stool pigeons around without you." He loves nonliterary language and isn't ashamed to use it. He imagines informers everywhere, and I think he has good reason. He's a daring man and not on the best terms with the authorities. Tanya wept and through her tears said piteously, "You have to understand, I'm tired of being alone. Whatever he is, at least he's a man."

"He can go fuck himself," the writer said. "You're better off alone." I agree.

DECEMBER 6. People combat loneliness in different ways. Natasha is the eternal type of Russian woman, courageous, radiant, and infinitely kind. She would have made an ideal wife and mother, but life didn't arrange it. She lives with her parents, to whom she gives all her spiritual warmth. She is tall, slender, and feminine, with blue eyes, light hair, and a childlike pout. She is shy and indecisive, but these traits hide a will of iron and an ability to work hard. Even on her days off Natasha gets up at six and goes to work. Along with her main job as an engineer, she has a second job for her soul, as she puts it. She leads tours to places connected to the lives of famous writers. In preparing such an excursion, she reads everything about the writer, gets archival materials, and moves into his era. He becomes a friend and idol for her, and Natasha can quote endless excerpts from his works.

Now Natasha is studying Russian Orthodox monasteries. She travels to various cities when time allows, goes to services, reads the Bible. Recently she sat down with her mother and said, "Do you want me to try out the monastic life on you?" For four hours she talked about the joy of serving God, about earthly temptations awaiting people at every step.

Natasha never talks about her temptations, but we know that she's had affairs. From the little she's said, I learned that they sought solace and help from her, and she naturally gave it. How could they have missed such a wonderful woman?

DECEMBER 8. Dasha told me an incredible thing that happened to a friend of hers. Lika is an extravagant Moscow intellectual in her forties. She's been married twice and has a grown daughter. She likes adventure and is attractive to men. A femme fatale.

The night before last Lika went to a major theatrical premiere. She didn't have a ticket, but usually people come up and offer to sell her one. This time another "ticketless" person, a handsome and respectable-looking man, hung around her. Despite their efforts, they couldn't get tickets, and they got into a conversation as they walked down the boulevard. He turned out to be learned, witty, and charming. Lika didn't feel like going home. She was glad to accept his offer of a cup of coffee. It's banal, but it's life. They had coffee, good Georgian wine, music. It was a wonderful night, everything done with attention and taste. In the morning he tenderly kissed her farewell out in the hall and asked if she regretted the night she had spent with him and if he had made her happy. She said she hadn't been that happy in a long time. He embraced her neck and artfully undid her gold chain. He took the necklace and said, "You have to pay for your pleasure, my dear." She couldn't believe her ears. He opened the door, put his arm around Lika's waist, and led her to the elevator. She went downstairs and out onto the street in shock. Nothing like this had ever happened to her. She'd had arguments and curses hurled at her, but Lika had never seen such a refined scoundrel.

DECEMBER 10. Katya's dream has come true. She recently met a Frenchman working in Moscow. It would be perfect except for the language problem. He doesn't speak Russian; she doesn't speak French. She barely knows English, and his English is little better. Today she came to me for help in basic phrases. The idea is to show him that she is a serious, positive young woman who is not interested in one-night stands. In other words, either intend marriage or get the hell out. But it has to be said delicately, by innuendo, and in grammar, the subjunctive is the most difficult. I wrote out entire sentences for her. She is talented when it comes to men. We'll see what happens. We decided that if he doesn't understand, I'll be brought in to help. If he pretends not to understand a thing, I'll bring my dubious French into play.

They're going to the ballet tonight. She's tempting him with the full intellectual program: museums, theaters, concerts. Everyone has her own way of winning happiness. I think that Katya's isn't the worst.

DECEMBER 11. I've stopped writing about myself lately. There's nothing to write: the usual gray, dull stuff and loneliness. Besides, I don't have the strength for passion; it always ends sadly. I guess I shouldn't take it so seriously. The poet Bella Akhmadulina, whom I admire so much, has a marvelous poem about how she sometimes wants to be a frivolous coquette from the last century, but it is not her fate. She must sing the praises of those marvelous specters. All I can do is envy them.

In olden days there were many words to describe a man's courtship of a woman. They reflected the various nuances and degrees of seriousness. He's "following her around" meant a sweet and slightly frivolous attention that promised nothing. No one thinks in those terms now, the whole concept has died out. Before he "wanted to be affianced," but now they say "he wants to propose." There was something respectful about being affianced. The man would come to the house, ask for the parents' permission, and wait anxiously for the young lady's acceptance. There was another nice expression; "ask for her hand." "Propose" or "make a proposal," as we put it now, sounds like a line from a contract. "Citizeness Ivanova, I want to make a proposal to you."

And there was the lovely tradition of posting the banns. Now, instead of that, people go to ZAGS, the registry office, and "submit an application," which sounds like a party committee meeting. And the church wedding has been replaced by "registering" the marriage.

I've started with the lighthearted "following her around" and ended with a wedding: dreaming again.

Nowadays men don't know how to court women. Instead, they just have quickie affairs. Men decided that if a woman flirts and gets their attention, she's looking for sex. Women are partially to blame for that. We're too much in a hurry. Of course, if you don't hurry, you'll be left all alone. The men have a simple

approach now: "If you don't want to, I'll go find someone else."
They always have a dozen phone numbers to spare.

We have a friend, an elderly and impressive pilot, who has
sown his wild oats and has lovely memories. He likes to sit in
his armchair with a snifter of cognac and a cigar and talk about
love. "Men cheat themselves today. They deprive themselves of
the best part of love—courtship. A woman must be conquered,
cleverly, inventively, beautifully. There's no interest if she gives
herself to you the first night. The harder the battle, the sweeter
the victory." Then he gives examples from his life. I listen to
him and think, *Where are you, valiant conquerors? Why do we
have to deal only with impatient consumers?*

DECEMBER 12. My neighbor Masha needs no one. She has
a lovely daughter to whom she devotes all her attention and
love. Masha can do everything: make money, do repairs in the
apartment, sew, knit, cook, fix the TV. I know that life alone
isn't easy for her, but she never complains. She's created an
image of herself that everyone accepts. When she has suitors
from time to time, she hurries to assure me that she doesn't
need them. Our apartments are at an angle, so we can see into
each other's kitchens. "Sasha spent the night?" I ask the next
morning. "Why do you ask? You saw him sleeping on the cot
in the kitchen," Masha replies. When one of us has a guest, the
other is bursting with curiosity.

Occasionally Masha decides that it's time to find a good
father for her daughter, but that passes quickly since there are
no candidates.

And so we sit in her kitchen, she with a cigarette, I with a cup of tea, talking about nothing, looking at her new clothes.

DECEMBER 15. Dasha's artist turned out to be a creepy egoist. He exhausted her. She sat in my kitchen and cried today. She had waited a whole hour at the exhibit for him, and when he arrived, he told her that he had to discuss a problem with his friends. She had been planning a pleasant evening for just the two of them. He was like that all the time: Either he showed up unexpectedly, full of love, or he couldn't find five minutes to talk on the phone. "I still love him," Dasha said through her tears. "He's so talented and smart, I'm ready to forgive him anything."

"Dasha, remember, you said the same thing about Viktor just three months ago," I reminded her.

"I remember, but now I'm in love with the artist."

I swear, sometimes I envy Dasha.

DECEMBER 17. Today Katya came to visit, chicly dressed in a new American coat that she bought from a friend. She looks marvelous, but she's totally bewildered. Her friend Ira recently came back from Holland to visit her parents. She's been living for several years with her husband, a successful businessman. She told Katya all about how boring life is in the West. You may have everything, but your heart is heavy. Her first husband was the son of a famous Moscow writer. They lived a merry bohemian life, with endless guests, champagne, and interesting conversation. Holland is just a measured bourgeois life. Her husband works a lot, comes home tired, and sits in his chair drinking beer and watching TV. In Moscow Ira's new clothes were a sensation, but in Holland she's just like everyone else. Her euphoria from living in the West is over, and Ira is sad. She's plunged into Moscow's night life and is in no hurry to go back. Last night Katya and Ira had a lot to drink, and Ira laughingly recounted the scene she recently had with her husband. They came home after a boring formal party, and she began to complain about local life. Her husband, always understanding and kind, tried to console her, making her even crazier. It ended with him on his knees begging her to forgive him for who knew what, and she slapped him on the face and shouted, "You boring Dutch burgher, you'll never understand the mysterious Russian soul."

Ira's friends told Katya in secret that when her husband is away on business, Ira often heads for Amsterdam's dubious areas and deals with her Russian ennui in a very frivolous manner.

"I want to go to the West so much," Katya said. "But what if I'm not happy there either?"

"First of all, no one's invited you there yet, and secondly, it depends on what you want out of life," I replied soundly. Really, it's stupid to go to the West for clothing and fun. People have their own problems there. Someone should tell Ira's husband to give her less money and make her get a job. She'd have less time to be bored.

Katya and I talked and decided that she shouldn't worry ahead of time, counting her chickens before they're hatched or, as we say in Russia, dividing up the fur of an unkilled bear. And until she leaves for Europe, she can go around and kill her suitors with her new American coat.

DECEMBER 19. We're having a late autumn this year, still no snow. The day is foggy and not cold. Natasha and I went for a walk. I like walking on days like this. The world seems small and cozy. I'm lucky to live in such a marvelous neighborhood— the river, a small village, a big park with an eighteenth-century church. It's hard to believe that all this is in a city. The authorities keep threatening to take down the little village and build another dozen ugly high rises. The village is not in anyone's way. And it supplies the whole neighborhood with greens and fruit; the locals grow cucumbers, green onions, and parsley, which they sell at the market. In the fall almost all our apples come from there.

We walked around the village. The streets were empty because most people stay home in weather like this. The trees are bare, and the wooden fences dark gray in the damp. The occasional light blue house with white window frames pleases the eye. Our late autumn is sorrowful. How much love, depression, poetry, and hopelessness have these autumn days. And that humid autumnal air bears a million scents—half of Russia in it.

Natasha and I wandered in the park, walking to the half-ruined wooden house from the last century. The lovely building is slowly falling apart. I like to imagine the house filled with people drinking tea on the big veranda, piano music and love songs coming through the window. I'd love to look through the cracks in the shutters, but I'm afraid. It must be all empty and abandoned with only the wind howling inside.

We went to the church, which, despite everything, is in pretty good shape. The revolutionary storm passed it by. It's locked up, too, of course, and all the icons and church vestments were stolen long ago. It stands in the middle of the dreary autumn like a lovely pearl that no one wants. Guidebooks call it a masterpiece of Russian architecture.

Natasha (this is another, younger Natasha) is agitated but happy. She is pregnant. She has wanted a baby for many years, but it never happened. Now that her dream has come true, she's having doubts. The times are so troubled and uncertain, and they live with her in-laws in a small apartment with no hope of getting their own place.

Natasha is a specialist in literature, a wise and subtle woman. We talk about books, the new prose, the fate of writers who left. She can't imagine a life for herself outside Russia, even though she suffers from our horrors. She wants to pass on her love of Russian literature to her future child, to bring up a truly educated and honest person. I agree with her, but a child like that will have a terribly difficult time surviving amid the general disillusionment and aggression.

But her main concern now is the baby's health. Most of the maternity hospitals are full of infection, and the mothers bring home children who then need to be treated for staph infection for several months. Natasha is also afraid of childbirth. Her friends have told her all sorts of horrors about maternity homes and their lack of medicine, linens, and elementary conveniences. The women don't even have a place to wash up. After giving birth, one friend had to spend another two hours on a stretcher in the birthing room because there was no room in the ward. She said she practically gave birth a second time with the others. It's only after she started having hysterics that the staff noticed her and moved her.

Natasha is looking for friends who could get her into a decent maternity home where the doctor would get to know her and attend the birth. Everyone's trying to do that.

As I walked, I was glad I didn't have these problems. I don't even mean myself so much as the baby. Giving birth in those conditions and into a world of complete uncertainty is almost criminal. I decided long ago that one can't have children in our country today. Even with my more or less established life, what could I give a child? How could I teach it to be happy when I'm always on the verge of despair?

Of course, deep in my heart I envy Natasha, but I just can't do it myself.

DECEMBER 21.   Dasha is fine now. Her affair with the artist is in full swing despite his tricks. She is still in love and prepared to put up with him, but I know that she'll be sick of him soon.

Events for Katya are developing at breakneck speed. The Frenchman has proposed. Everything went according to the best traditions of European life: He gave her a diamond ring and asked for her hand at dinner at her parents' home. Katya, of course, has forgotten her worries and is no longer afraid of life in the West. The Frenchman is going home now and will be back in a few weeks on a new project; then they will marry. Katya is in seventh heaven.

DECEMBER 22. Maybe I'll try marriage again. Find a good husband and live a quiet measured life like . . . who? Really, which of my friends is happily married? I went through them all, and incredible as it may seem, I couldn't come up with one inspiring example. There's a good Russian proverb: "The women complain; the girls are willing to get married." Really, half my friends either have never married or are divorced and wouldn't mind marrying again. The other half, who are married, seem to envy us. Recently a friend of Mama's said, "I sometimes wonder whose daughter is happier, mine or yours? Mine seems to have everything—a good husband, a daughter, money, a car. But she works like a slave from morning until night. The garden at the dacha alone is so much work. And yours is strolling around Munich, seeing the world, and living for herself." I have always looked at her daughter with envy. She seems so prosperous and happy in our world, which is so complicated for women. I remember that Socrates said, "It's bad for a man to marry, and it's bad not to." I think this applies to women as well.

CHAPTER SIX 🌿

A Job's a Job

A job's not a wolf; it won't run away into the woods.
—RUSSIAN PROVERB

DECEMBER 23. Oh, how I hate getting up early. A gray, gloomy sky, drizzling rain . . . I could sleep and sleep. Life seems hopeless at moments like this. All you can think about is hopping back into your warm bed. I always loll in bed to the very last second, then leap out, shower, dress, have a glass of tea, and run to the trolley. If I don't make that trolley I may be late for my lecture. I run the fifty-meter dash, coat flapping in the wind, hat askew, but I climb aboard. Sometimes I get a seat, and I have another fifteen minutes to wake up fully and concentrate on the coming lecture. The students are always as sleepy as I am, so I have to start with a few jokes. To tell the truth, I'm often in no mood for jokes; I'm grumpy and grim. On days like this I allow myself to say, "I don't feel like working any more than you do, so let's make an effort together." I'd be happy to have the lecture canceled for a so-called discussion with the other teachers, especially with the chief. He likes to solo, and I can doze with a wise look on my face. The main trick is to pretend to be fully participating, nodding occasionally, making an assenting gesture now and then. Out of politeness the chief sometimes turns to me and says, "Don't you think so?" I'm not even listening. I sneak looks at my watch. But when I have to lecture, I have to concentrate.

I jump down from the trolley and run with the crowd to the metro. I don't always get a seat there. I'm lucky if the car's not stuffed to the gills. Lately I've developed real claustrophobia; I can't ride in a crowded car. If the train stops in the tunnel between stations, I get panicky and can't breathe, and I start pushing people to get a little space around me.

Then another small marathon to my job. It's easy enough in the spring and summer, but when it's icy and snowy, it's a real hassle. The snow isn't cleared and forms a thick layer of slippery, bumpy ice. I've developed a special walk—legs far apart and body tilted forward. At times like that I hope I won't meet anyone I know.

I think I'm not late, and there's time to freshen up. The workday starts. After the lecture I have to hurry to the canteen, which is open for only fifteen minutes during the breaks. If I see a familiar face in the line, I squeeze in. The first small pleasures of the day are there: hot coffee, tasty sandwiches.

There was a faculty meeting today, so I had to hang around until three. There are always a lot of petty chores: take away some papers; order photocopies; confirm the schedule. There are friends in every room, so it may take up to two hours. Our staff mysteriously vanishes now and then, even though there are only two corridors. It's important to create the illusion of activity. If you're not in your office, you must be on urgent business. If you stay at your desk reading or writing for a long time (as is almost impossible in our microscopic room), it almost looks as if you don't have anything to do. The administrators will come up with something for sure, so it's better to keep moving. If there is something urgent, the chief grabs the first person he sees. If you're not in the room, you're saved. But you have to show up every half hour or so just to confirm your existence.

I learned these tricks only after two or three years on the job. Up to then I had nothing but trouble. The boss was always getting me. Now I am as elusive as the others. It's easy for the smokers. They're always out in the hall; there's a kind of club out there.

Two hours slipped by unnoticed, and lunchtime came. Lunch is the peak of the workday. We have a good lunchroom, and the food is tasty. After lunch, when you feel relaxed and indifferent, the desire to be back home in bed is almost irresistible. Three o'clock finally rolled around, but we couldn't get organized. Somebody was in the canteen; someone was smoking; someone else was on the phone. No one wanted to have the meeting, but we had to. It passed peacefully today without arguments or fights and ended almost at six o'clock. I had to race to the metro before the rush hour. The way home is always happier.

I came home, undressed, and flopped in an armchair. Why am I so tired? I didn't really do much. My only real work was the lecture, which lasted only ninety minutes.

DECEMBER 24. When will she leave me alone? My very presence irritates her. It's a very simple explanation: envy. A lot of people think that I have a happy and carefree life. I don't complain about men; I don't get angry when someone else has a new dress; I don't borrow three rubles until payday. And my personal life has been kept secret from them. Naturally that annoys them. But this lady is going beyond all bounds. On my birthday I came to work in a fur jacket. No one could understand why our faculty meeting was so stormy; everything drove her crazy. It's funny, but the reason, as I later learned, was my jacket.

When our workdays coincide, I try to wear old clothing. Why upset her and me? She even keeps an eye on what I order in the lunchroom, and one day she commented that I was having a very expensive meal.

The worst thing is that she won't let me work. All my suggestions and ideas are rejected outright. However small my contribution to scholarship could be, it is blocked by steaks, blouses, and skirts.

Of course, I understand that her life is difficult. She is losing her youth and attractiveness, but what do I have to do with that?

I've come to the conclusion that there are two kinds of people: those who release their tensions at work and those who leave their bad moods at home. Life is easier for the former; they are feared at work and loved at home. I tried losing my temper at work a few times. It was magic. Everyone pays attention to you; no one pesters you with chores; everyone wants to be on your good side. The only thing you lose is your self-respect. Academician Likhachev once defined a representative of the intelligentsia as one who doesn't interfere with other people's lives.

I'm afraid to talk about the second group of people because I think I belong in it. I often come home tired and grumpy, and I know that I should control myself, but alas . . . It's written all over my face as soon as I enter the apartment. According to

Likhachev's definition, I'm not one of the intelligentsia because I'm ruining the lives of the people closest to me.

There is a small and sad justification, of course. Work inevitably puts me in a bad mood. The bureaucratic system gives rise to total disrespect for a person. "They" know what is best for you; you are helpless. Even if you start to fight, the result is always the same: You lose. Then how can you come home in a good mood?

DECEMBER 25. The new law on alcohol has spoiled everyone's lives. You can't drink at the office! There were so many fun days in the year—a few revolutionary holidays, International Women's Day, New Year's, plus at least five or six birthdays. People brought good food, bottles of cognac and wine, a cake and sat down and forgot their squabbles. Really, for a not very congenial Soviet collective, we did well. After we had drunk in our room, we went to visit the next one, the neighbors came to ours, and then we all went to the nearest store for more wine. After a few hours we were really buddies. The rumor said that the bosses drank in their offices. You could get a clear picture of office politics and power plays by who was invited to join them.

Now everyone's fighting drunkenness! It doesn't bother me, but I'm sorry for the others. Of course, you can drink secretly and quickly, but then you can't give in to the high in public (you can be fired even for a whiff of alcohol on your breath). You have to sneak downstairs and home. As for the "techniques of pouring," the Soviet people are infinitely inventive. They banned cognac at the officers' mess of one military garrison. The counter woman found a solution right away: She poured cognac into tea glasses, and to make things look realistic, she gave them a couple of cubes of sugar and a teaspoon in the saucer. The officers were happy because they got two hundred grams instead of fifty in each glass.

Despite all the antialcohol severity, curious things still happen. A watchman went to check the rooms and found the office manager dead drunk. It scared the old watchman, who had been unable to open the door since the drunk's legs had been propped against it. Another story was spicier. Two staff members were found in a classroom. When the door was opened, he started running around in search of his trousers, but she was too happily high to worry. Both were fired. Before, drunkenness was considered a minor human fault, for which people were chided but not punished. Now it's all different. I think it's gotten better. There are fewer drunkards on the street, and you don't smell alcohol on your fellow passengers in the metro and bus.

DECEMBER 26. Sometimes it's not so bad to go to work. Quite often it's a substitute for everything else—a women's club (which we don't have), store, beauty salon, and literary salon. We have plenty of free time, so we get together with the charming girls from another room and discuss men, sex, fashion, and health. In contrast with American women, we don't discuss recipes. If we do talk about food, it's only where to buy it. Cooking it is a secondary consideration.

One of our favorite topics is putting down men for being

egotistical, lazy bums and scoundrels. All of us have examples from our own lives, and any thesis can be supported with convincing facts. Recently Irina's boyfriend went off with another, and she's still upset. We keep telling her that she'll find someone else. Olya's husband refuses to earn money and told her, "Why should I support you? You have an education, too." Lyuda's husband won't sleep with her (this is not widely known). Nadya's husband, on the other hand, wants her all the time. I prefer to listen. It's not interesting to talk about my ex-husband. But we never run out of material, and sometimes we even stay after work.

Some of the women have special talents—sewing, knitting, cutting hair. Work is where we order and try on dresses and blouses and have our hair done and get manicures and massages.

However, our biggest amusement is buying and selling clothing. We get valuable information at work about what's on sale where, and we can order deficit goods. Say one woman sees French nail polish in the morning. We quickly chip in, send her to the store, and cover for her absence. Men sometimes participate in these games, too. Recently we sent a young professor to buy American makeup kits. We lost on that one because you could buy only two per person. His wife got one; his boss, the other.

Certain goods arrive directly from abroad. Some of the girls have friends working there. The girls do a small business helping sell the things their friends bring back. The clothing isn't from Dior, but it's not from the neighborhood department store either.

I remember a story Mama told. The principal of her school had a great sense of humor. Watching the women examining an imported bra, he said, "Girls, if it doesn't fit any of you, I'll take it." But seriously, men buy things for their wives at work, too.

DECEMBER 28. I love my job when I'm actually doing it. It's the enforced lying and doing nothing that I hate. But what else could I do? Disregard everything? I'd be eaten alive. You have to be an irreplaceable specialist or have nerves of steel. Unfortunately neither applies to me. How can you become a professional when you have to lecture on more than twenty topics? We are "broad-profile" specialists, jacks-of-all-trades, masters of none. We often joke among ourselves as we head off to the lecture hall: "Which will we do this time—sing or dance?" We manage on our general erudition and favorite topics. That's also an art, starting a conversation on economics, for instance (what the lesson plan calls for), and then steering it ten minutes later to the mysterious phenomena of the human mind. It's hard to talk about concrete problems because no one knows what to do about them. It's better to stick to the eternal topics: literature, mysticism, love.

Students have changed in recent years. They used to swallow everything. They read newspapers, knitted, or talked during bad lectures. Now they don't want to knit or read. They want to hear the truth. Why must we pay for the sins of others by standing in confusion before our audience? We're still afraid to tell the whole truth, and no one needs half-truths anymore. Naïve students are expecting concrete advice from us. Where are we supposed to get it? It's impossible to teach theory because it differs from practice, and practice differs from common sense.

Smart students either skip lectures or don't ask questions and gladly chat about interesting topics.

I think that what's important now is learning how to talk freely and without fear about everything—politics, concerns and cares, feelings, disappointments. The "inner censor" is still inside each of us, and I doubt that our generation will ever be free of it.

No, in our troubled times the best thing is to teach something like ancient history or archaeology. There's a funny joke. On the final exam in Marxism-Leninism the teacher can't get any answers from a student. He finally asks the easiest question: "Who were Marx and Engels?"

"I don't know," the student replies.

"And Lenin?"

"I don't know either."

The teacher is stunned. "Where did you come from, dear fellow, what remote corner of the world?"

"From the city of Kozlov."

The teacher gives him a D and then goes to the window, looks out into the distance, and says softly, "I wonder, should I say the hell with everything and move to Kozlov?"

DECEMBER 29. How can you run off when there's such a great canteen, such a great lunchroom, as well as clean toilets and carpet runners in the halls? At my last job the lunchroom stank unbearably, and we had to stand in line for forty minutes to gulp down disgusting food in the remaining five.

Here we treat special perks with great respect. When the

canteen is offering deficit products like meat, fish, or cottage cheese, we drop whatever we're doing and hurry down. The canteen is more important than anything else. "He's in the canteen" is as impressive as "He's lecturing." We hurry after the ones already there. When coffee vanished from the city, everyone came into work, even on days off, for a cup or two. Our canteen feeds not only those who work here but their relatives and friends. I managed to feed a friend's sick dog; I bought liver, which the dog loved. People go home from work with large shopping bags filled with food.

Back in the thirties the satiric writers Ilf and Petrov captured the rapidly developing reality of Soviet life: "Beer only for union members." That's why you need a pass to get into our institute. We have no state secrets, but we do have our canteen. It's no wonder that we calculate the effectiveness of our workday by the amount of products we buy. And here we have true equality. Professor and cleaning woman are equally happy to buy a stick of sausage. Actually, the professor may be even happier because he doesn't have a lot of time to shop. He has to lecture as well.

We're so used to this that we don't even notice the absurdity of our life!

There's a marvelous story on the subject. A writer exiled from the Soviet Union is riding in a cab in New York and talking about Moscow life with the driver. "Tell me, do you really have problems with food? What's it like?" the cabby asks.

"It's like this," the writer replies. "Just imagine that you get up early in New York, go to the station, get into a crowded train. You arrive in Washington a few hours later, run around the stores all day, and finally find a stick of sausage, naturally not the kind you'd like, but sausage nevertheless. You come back to New York that evening, exhausted but happy."

The cabdriver couldn't get it. And really, how do you explain it to a New York cabby?

DECEMBER 30. I think I've defeated my tormentor. Lately she's been truly intolerable. She went to all the rooms and told a fantastic lie about me: that I was practically an underground millionaire. If only that were true! I was doubly hurt because I'm having financial problems right now.

I picked a moment when we were alone, and I let her have it. I told her that I wouldn't put up with her nonsense anymore and that I was declaring war. A few days later she turned into my best friend and defender. With friends like that who needs enemies? But this was a lesson for me, although a dangerous one. If you start fighting people like that with their own weapons, you won't even notice becoming one of them. Of course, our whole system is built on that: Be like everyone else, part hypocrite, part intriguer, part deceiver, and in total a simple, open, and unobtrusive Soviet person.

JANUARY 2, 1989. As there is everywhere else, there are love stories at work. There are lonely women and local lotharios. Students fall in love with teachers, and teachers with students. Students here are adults, so there's nothing necessarily bad about it. We already have one happily wedded couple.

One of our young men falls only for tall brunettes. Another likes all pretty women and, according to reliable sources, has already slept with four and wanted to marry two (even though he's already married). His affairs have led to touchy moments and scenes of jealousy in the halls. One seduced and abandoned girl, suspecting nothing, bawled on the shoulder of her replacement. The girls shared sweet, intimate details about him. They could have held a scholarly symposium on that man.

The most unpredictable people are lonely women. Periods of frenzied work alternate with episodes of mysterious love. The work attacks are harmful to the rest; they sweep everyone out of their path. On the love days they are dreamy and lovely. They float down the hallways (despite their girth), smile at everyone, and forget their heightened work discipline of a few days ago.

The most dangerous people are the lonely, jealous women when they fall in love with staff members. Then you have to keep away from their chosen ones, even on business. They'll turn you to ash with their gazes, make up lies, and avenge themselves over nothing. So you have to be aware and keep up with the romance department to stay out of trouble. We have women who know all. You can come to them at any moment for the information you seek. When you're in a bad mood, you can ask them to fill you in on someone. It's like a soap opera. You can forget your own problems and follow someone else's life drama.

When I was getting a divorce, I didn't tell anyone because I knew that my problems could become someone else's amusement.

To tell the truth, I enjoy good gossip myself. Sometimes, if we don't finish stories at work, we call each other in the evenings.

I have my "agents" who gather my information (what the boss said about me, what others replied, and so on). Naturally I spy on their behalf, but bear in mind that there is counterespionage at work, too, like the KGB and the CIA with all their departments.

JANUARY 3. About ten years ago what I am writing here would have been enough to put me in prison or have me declared insane and fired. Just for describing my life and my feelings! And there's a whole generation like me. A recent sociological poll tried to paint a portrait of various generations. My generation was dropped; a ten-year period was skipped. I guess there's nothing to say about us; we're nothing. Or perhaps nothing unites us besides emptiness and apathy. Everyone survived in his or her own way.

We caught a piece of the Khrushchev thaw when we were children. Our parents took us along when they went to visit friends—not to party and drink but to read Khrushchev's letter to the Twentieth Congress of the Communist party or Yevtushenko's autobiography. We'd get home late at night (those retyped pages would be available only for one evening), and I'd imagine Black Marias on every street corner. I am grateful to my parents that they did not spare my young mind or imagination. They knew that I'd never be a young builder of communism anyway, and knowing the truth was painful but necessary. I was allowed to read banned adult books, and they spoke frankly about politics at the dinner table.

Despite the grim revelations, the Khrushchev times were

filled with naïve and sincere optimism. People danced the twist, drank wine, fell in love, went to literary evenings, read poetry, and believed in the future, though, of course, not the radiant Communist one. I watched my older cousin enviously when she put on dresses with full skirts and went off to dances. I waited for my turn, but it never came.

Our high school and university years were different. We were again stuffed with Marxism-Leninism; we were again told that Stalin hadn't been so bad, that he had raised the country out of ruin and created a world power. But I knew better. . . . Studying at an elite Soviet college, I was surrounded by the children of bureaucrats—the luxuriously dressed girls and the obnoxious boys who were driven to school in black Volgas. Sometimes they made me feel inferior, for I dressed modestly. It was hard for a professor's daughter to compete in that area with the daughter of a Central Committee chauffeur.

We were plunging headlong into the era of Brezhnev corruption. It was a time of total permissiveness for some and total hopelessness for others. Money could buy anything—an African lion, a trip to New York, a Hero of the Soviet Union star. And at the same time you couldn't go visit friends in Poland or Hungary, you couldn't correspond with Americans, you couldn't read Solzhenitsyn. When I returned from the house of a Dutch friend (that was daring, having a friend like that in Moscow) with a copy of *The Gulag Archipelago* in my bag, I was risking everything—my father's job and career, my future. There were many incidents when people were approached in the metro, taken into a room, and searched. A relative of a friend of mine got caught like that. As a precautionary measure, my friend's family "evacuated" their dissident library from their home to the country and waited for a search that luckily did not come.

We were afraid of one another. Our small crowd at college had two snitches: one out of conviction, the other out of need (he had almost been expelled for bad grades).

We walked with horror past the Serbsky Institute, where political prisoners were kept. What could be more terrible than a healthy person's being forcibly and painfully treated in a psychiatric hospital?

An entire family paid for an incorrect move from the Soviet regime's point of view. If a young woman married a foreigner, the father was fired from work. A sister's happiness depended on the unhappiness of her brother. People were afraid to have anything to do with émigré relatives. They hated themselves for it, but they had to survive.

Of course, compared with Stalinist times, this was heaven. We went to sleep knowing that we would wake up in our own beds. Life went on. It's just that we were dying inside, unnoticed, drop by drop, every day.

In our leisure time my girl friends and I preferred to sleep. We never called each other before eleven on Sunday. In my dreams I often traveled to other countries. I have clear memories of the Eiffel Tower and the cathedral in Cologne, and I stood and wept, unable to believe that it was true. We were served up a romantic song as consolation for us: "Don't be sad, friend, about Paris. Look, the Siberian taiga is all around us. You can have Montmartre by a camp fire and tea instead of cognac," and so on. By the way, the singer eventually emigrated to Israel or America.

Sheremetyevo International Airport was like the gateway

to the world, a gate you could never go through. Some of my friends went there to eat in the cafeteria. You could have a sausage sandwich and hear "Moscow-London, Moscow-Paris, Moscow-New York." Masochism! We had a silly joke back then. "I want to go to Paris again."

"When were you in Paris?"

"Never. It's just that I wanted to go yesterday, too."

Of course, our only salvation lay in a sense of humor. We fantasized and made up funny stories and laughed until we cried. There was something hysterical about it.

Nevertheless, we expected a miracle. Everything would change, and a normal, human life would begin. However, we knew that the only real miracle would be to go abroad. We dreamed of a handsome prince (not necessarily with blue balls) who would take us away over the Alps or across the ocean. What about my parents, though? I'd wake up at night and think: *No, I can't leave, no, never, I'll manage here somehow.*

JANUARY 8. I loved my first job. It was wonderful and a tormenting illusion of another life. Almost every day I spent time with foreigners who told me about their lives and gave me books and magazines. They were exactly like me; it was just that they had been born in another country. And every time they flew off to what I considered their happy planet, I had to stay in the "Communist paradise." We went on living in our country, which we loved but in which we felt unneeded and damned.

It was only recently that we began speaking about the values of human life and about the right to happiness. The word "charity" had been struck from the dictionaries as a bourgeois concept. Only a few years ago we saw that our lives were worth nothing, that every day dozens or hundreds of young men were dying senselessly in Afghanistan. I hated and loved my country, afraid to leave it but no longer able to live in it. I wasn't so sure that I would be happy "out there." The word "homeland," made trite and cheap by Soviet slogans, had meaning for me.

I paid for my double life. Often, as I saw off another group to their inaccessible world, I'd weep uncontrollably. I didn't know how I could go on living. I had no ground under my feet. The poet's line came back to haunt us decades later: "We live not feeling the country beneath us."

JANUARY 9. At long last I can live on my salary, I think. It's considered impolite to ask about salary when you're applying for a job. You're supposed to feel that the joy of free Communist labor is reward enough. The rest is your parents' worry. There's even a joke on the matter. "His parents are so irresponsible. They can't take care of him until he retires." Of course, my prosperity is also illusory, and most of my big expenses have been covered by my parents.

When you start counting up and comparing, you feel sad and ridiculous. I've worked for so many years, and my salary is only slightly over 200 rubles a month. If you figure it in dollars, it's around $40 a month, even less on the black market. Of course, it's hard to make a real comparison. Our apartments are inexpensive, and so is public transportation. You can buy a loaf of bread for 20 kopecks. Basically you won't starve, and you can even buy a pair of winter boots in a month, if you don't eat. But how do the people making 120 rubles a month manage?

Every day we see wonderful examples of Soviet social justice parading by our office—fat speculators in luxurious Western duds. There used to be a commissary, or secondhand store, here which sold Western electronics. The store was moved to another location, but the speculators remained. They have an open-air office. When it's cold, they work out of their cars. There's no such thing as a speculator without a car.

We're work neighbors. They know the girls from our place and say hello every morning. The girls earn five or ten rubles a day while the chic boys make several hundred or even thousand a day. The "boys" (some of them pushing sixty) have good on-the-job protection. Once a young inexperienced policeman came over to them and asked about their profession. The policeman was told never to show his face there again if he wanted to keep his job. Of course, the boys do end up in jail from time to time. Often it's their "colleagues" who arrange it. As a rule, they don't stay in long and come back enriched by the life experience. The major speculators, I've heard, often pick up a new job inside; they become professional stoolies. I saw one once. He drove around Moscow in a fancy Western car, a real European gentleman.

There are marvelous stories told about them. One millionaire was arrested over a deal that called for him to bring a briefcase with goods valued at about two thousand rubles to the next building. He did it for a thrill, and they got him. The speculators are tough cookies. They control the best restaurants, where only foreigners are allowed. When they see a beautiful woman, they invite her date out into the lobby and offer him a caseful of money, just to leave the lady on her own.

So our neighbors are wonderful and inspire us in our joyous free labor.

JANUARY 11. My diary seems awfully gloomy—just wastrels disillusioned with life or fat-cat speculators. I'm put off by it myself.

After all, there are talented, wise, and noble people. At our institute we have several brilliant teachers who give marvelous lectures and write books. It's funny, but almost all of them are bearded and wear glasses, the traditional image of the Russian intellectual.

Russia was famous for its excellent professors. Unfortunately almost none of them remain, for the old generation is gone and there are only a few individuals in the new.

Coeds traditionally fall in love with these teachers. When I was at college, we had several idols. Their lectures were beauty contests for us. We all put on fresh makeup and fixed our hair in the breaks and naturally had no time to prepare the lessons. My girl friend and I were part of the general madness. We made sure we were the last ones for the oral exam with the most inaccessible and smart professor. We tried to overwhelm him with our charm and certain knowledge of the subject. Neither was enough. He gave us each a C and suggested we learn the sound correlations in the Indo-European languages. Blinded by love, we didn't even notice our bad grades, and instead of studying for the next exam, we followed our idol around the institute. As a result, we both got C's on the next exam, too.

Incidentally that specialist on Indo-European languages later married a student.

JANUARY 18. Now here's a story in reverse. Today I had another date with my former student. The word "student" is rather misleading since he is older than I am and could be my teacher.

I admit that this whole affair was my doing. I figured everything out accurately to the very day. But what if he had been doing his own calculations?

All right, if this is an intimate diary, then all my secrets must be out on the table. I saw him last year, when he came to our office on business. He was an attractive young man, educated and well brought up. As people say, "I noticed him," because it's important to have a reserve of potential admirers, especially in Moscow, where they're in such short supply.

Six months passed. I was gradually returning to life after the divorce, and I remembered Aleksandr, Sasha for short. An excuse turned up, or I invented it, to discuss a scholarly article. The topic of my article just "happened" to coincide with his field. Things didn't go beyond several meetings at work and a trip to the movies. Of course, I wasn't in a rush.

Suddenly, O Providence, I ran into him at the institute, where he had come to study for a month. I quickly began finishing the article, and we saw each other every day. It was time to move on. I made a date for a particularly detailed discussion, and after it was over, I hinted that it was very hot and it would be nice to go for a walk in the park. He was afraid to cut classes. Was he a bore? Using my authority as an instructor, I subtly led him to the metro and told him that the best part of the park was near my house. Everything went according to plan, as if I were writing a novel.

After a marvelous walk you need to have tea, and I just happened to have a delicious cake I had baked the day before. "Don't be afraid, no one's at home except my turtle," I told him. He pretended to be politely hesitant.

It was a lovely summer day, all the windows wide open, and we sat in the kitchen and had tea. Then it was time for me to go to the pool. I changed into jeans and a T-shirt. We were in the hallway, ready to leave. Well, at last, he made up his mind! We kissed for a long time. It seemed that in skirt and blouse I was too much the teacher for him, and the jeans were the deciding factor. Should I go to the pool or not? We decided to meet the next day. What could be better than delicious anticipation?

The next day came, and many days after that. I think that people at work began to suspect. Sasha was always around me. I had a convenient schedule with a lot of free time, and he cut his classes. We spent wonderful days together, and were both paid a salary for it. There's one of the advantages of socialism.

Today we walked around the city. It started to rain, and we had to go into a crummy café. We sat drinking a sludge called pomegranate drink and holding hands. But I had to hold my breath because the café stank of revolting, burned food. It's not Paris, merely the center of Moscow.

Incidentally, the reviewer criticized my article. I wasn't upset. It played its part, and next time I'll write a good one.

JANUARY 19. I think I'm getting old. I've started comparing generations. "At your age we thought only about studying. We didn't wear makeup; we didn't sleep with boys." And it's true, I didn't use mascara until I was nineteen, I didn't have my first shot of cognac until I was eighteen, and my first kiss was at eighteen. Almost all the girls in my class were like that. There was one bohemian group, and their behavior was outrageous to us. We read American best sellers and had a theoretical knowledge of sex, but in real life sex was an exciting mystery. When one of our group got married, we asked her timorously, "Well, did you like it? Was it nice?" She said it wasn't bad but nothing special. We relaxed. We didn't sleep around because our parents had told us that you had to be a virgin when you got married.

The next generation was different. It adjusted better to cruel reality and matured early. There was a joke in the Armenian Radio series. "A grandmother calls in and asks if she should talk to her thirteen-year-old granddaughter about sex. Armenian Radio said that she should. She'd learn a lot that's new and interesting."

It's silly to lump everyone together, but the attitude of young people today is quite different. They quickly learned to take. They have nice clothes, have fun, and don't think about tomorrow. We gradually forgot how to work, but they never learned.

I'm probably overstating it, but I'm not criticizing them. I want to understand. Maybe I'm envious. The twenty-year-olds insouciantly flitting about at work delight me. They're a pleasure to look at, and they don't ruin other people's lives.

JANUARY 20. Joyous day—the end of the school semester, a few weeks ahead of legal indolence. Before the vacation we're told long and persistently that the next semester will be particularly important and significant and so on, so that we'll spend all two weeks thinking about how to work even better. But Soviets are experienced people. We've heard it all a hundred times— watershed, decisive, determining, completing year of the five-year plan. We know that they're all equally meaningless. It brings to mind a joke from the Brezhnev years. A middle-aged man comes home from work and tells his wife, "Starting tomorrow, our factory is going to work on a bidding plan."

"What's that?" his wife inquires.

"Just imagine that today I tell you that we're going to make love two times. And you reply, 'Three times,' even though we both know that we're lucky to manage even once."

CHAPTER SEVEN

Let's Sit Down, Friends, Before a Long Voyage

JANUARY 23. Foreigners are surprised and touched by our tradition of sitting down before leaving home on a trip. Everyone sits down for a minute in silence. Now people say it's to make sure you haven't forgotten anything; before, it was to say a prayer. And you're not supposed to sit near the stove; that will jinx the trip. Today we avoid sitting near the radiator.

Russians have always loved travel. It's in our blood. The theme of the road is strong in almost all the classics of the nineteenth century. Long trips are conducive to meditation, the Russian expanses and forests to poetic images and bittersweet sadness, and meetings on a journey to reminiscences and unexpected love affairs.

I'm off on a nostalgic ramble again. Let me get back to socialist reality. There was a popular joke in Brezhnev's day. An American and a Russian are comparing how many cars each family has. The American says, "We have one car for getting to work every day; it's small and practical. The other is for weekends and special occasions; it's bigger and fancier. And of course, we have the trailer for trips abroad, say, to Canada or Mexico."

"We don't need any cars at all," the Russian replied. "We

121

go to work by bus, to the country on weekends by railroad, and for special occasions we can splurge on a taxi."

"What about travel abroad?" the American asks.

"We use tanks."

It's a grim joke, with a grain of bitter truth, if we recall the events in Hungary, Czechoslovakia, and Afghanistan.

Ever since Stalin's day we have been cut off from the world, and trips abroad became a special privilege for functionaries. It was only in the early sixties that the curtain was lifted somewhat. Tours were arranged, and scientists and scholars were allowed to attend congresses and symposia. But every trip required the humiliating procedure of getting character references and other documentation.

Travel within the country was very complicated, too: lack of tickets, hotels, and other problems. What was meant to be pleasure turned into torture.

JANUARY 27. The "character reference" involves so many unpleasant associations. Until quite recently you couldn't take a trip abroad without one. Gradually its length diminished, and now, at last, it no longer exists. Originally it consisted of numerous questions that went back several generations. You had to list all relatives, including dead ones, where they lived and where they were buried. There was the question, Have you or any of your relatives lived in occupied territory? If you take into account the fact that a large part of the country had been occupied at one time or another by the Nazis, many people were under suspicion. If you had lived there, you had unlimited opportunities to become a spy, spend several decades lying low, and then plan to travel abroad in order to deliver the information you'd been gathering and return with a new assignment or else defect for capitalist goodies.

Of course, you had to be a shock worker, with busy public and social activism, and be politically literate. Also, you had to be characterized by moral stability—that is, not getting drunk and getting into fistfights on foreign territory or chasing the local beauties into your bed, and, most important, disappearing abroad. As a precaution, husbands and wives were not allowed to travel together. One always stayed behind as hostage.

Once you had the reference, which you often wrote yourself, you had to go from place to place, moving up the ladder, starting at work and ending up practically at the Central Committee of the party. At each place you were examined closely. Bureaucrats were looking for your potentially treacherous heart. After all, the desire to go abroad alone was suspicious in and of itself. You were asked a lot of unrelated questions. You had to know history, the political system of the country where you were planning to go, the names of its progressive political leaders and the heads of its Communist party, no matter how small and insignificant it might be. What if an ideological foe came up to you on the street? You'd have to be prepared with an educated and well-argued rebuff. There was a minor contradiction here: You were categorically discouraged from dealing with foreigners except for store clerks. And in general, you weren't allowed to walk around by yourself, just in case of a provocation or hostile act. There was a comedy in which a gawking Soviet tourist was dragged into an alleyway, knocked out, and given a cast with diamonds in the plaster. This comedy exposed the internal Mafia. After all, even Soviet society has its dregs.

Anyway, once you've gone through this whole rigmarole, you begin to doubt your own reliability. Before the trip you practice in front of a mirror, trying to look incredibly open and loyal to your Communist homeland. As you sit down before your voyage, you think, *Why do I have to go through all this torture? Why didn't I just go to the Black Sea in the Caucasus?*

JANUARY 29. But going to the Caucasus wasn't easy either. I have to tell the story of my trip to Tbilisi and Yerevan with my father. Papa's punctuality assured that the tickets were bought ahead of time, our route carefully planned, our supplies of maps and guidebooks well stocked. At the appointed hour we arrived respectably by taxi at the city air terminal for a bus to the airport. The scene before us cast us into despair. The huge terminal was stuffed with people. Almost all flights over the last few days had been canceled. The only information counter was under siege. At last we got an evasive answer: Wait. How long? An hour, two, a week?

"We don't know. Watch the announcement board." A few hours later the sign appeared announcing that the Tbilisi flight was delayed until tomorrow. My reasonable mother suggested turning in our tickets and getting rid of the headache. Papa and I decided not to give up. It had been so hard for me to get these ten days off. In Tbilisi were warm weather, a suite in the city's best hotel, and beloved friends.

We went home and called the terminal in the morning. We spent two fruitless hours on the phone and went back with our luggage to the announcement board. The situation had become even more heated. Unshaven, angry men wandered around the terminal. You can never get a hotel room in Moscow. Some threatened to send telegrams to the Central Committee; others simply cursed the Soviet regime. One intellectual-looking Georgian said furiously, "When I get home, I'll use one-hundred-ruble notes for wallpaper. That's all they're good for." Total freedom of expression reigned. It was like Hyde Park Corner without the comfort of Britain. Things were still unclear about our flight. There were no explanations. Various rumors circulated: bad weather (the skies were clear outside), no planes, no fuel. Papa and I had become as stubborn as madmen and held on to our tickets. We spent another night at home, and at last the next evening we heard what we had hoped for on the telephone. Registration had started for our flight. We grabbed our luggage, stole a taxi from under someone's nose, and rushed to the terminal. The news had been exaggerated: Registration was to start in another hour. Three hours later we were in the plane. It was dark outside, Papa was grim and taciturn, and we snapped at each other from time to time. Our voyage had begun.

Luckily the hotel had kept a room for us, but it wasn't a suite. We spent the first day regaining our senses. And a few days later the incredible happened: My teetotaling father got drunk. I think he just needed to get rid of his frustration. We went up into the mountains with some of my artist friends. It was still warm autumn below, but up there was snow, and it was cold. We went into a small, glassed-in café that didn't look like anything special. The stove glowed cozily inside, and the large wooden tables were quickly heaped with delicious Georgian foods and bottles of the famous wine. Our feast began. Compared with the hell of our last few days, we were in a magical kingdom. My friends made beautiful toasts to friendship, to our loved ones, to our departed. A noisy Georgian party celebrating the birth of a son started at the next table. Hearing that Papa and I were from Russia, they sent over a few more bottles of wine and raised toasts to us. We made speeches in return. This short-lived nonbinding warmth was so pleasant after the irritation and anger at the terminal.

Eventually everyone but our driver was drunk. We barely made it back to the car. A young man who would have been an heir (or almost an heir) to the Georgian throne if not for the Revolution was in charge of Papa. Prince Bagration was slightly more sober. In the car we sang, and Papa clapped hands and even tried to dance. I had never seen him like that. When we got to town, we stopped for a minute. The doors of the car opened, and my escorts and Papa fell in the bushes. The prince managed to get everyone back inside, and we headed for the hotel.

The next day Papa laughed and didn't believe my stories. Apparently I was the least drunk of the group and had the best recollection of the evening.

Then we went to Yerevan, a trip to ancient churches and monasteries. Father grew a bit sad and taciturn once more. His frustrations were still with him. At last we went home. Our friends took us to the airport in the morning, and once again there was unpleasant news: all flights to Moscow postponed indefinitely. The building was overcrowded, and there wasn't any place to sit. With difficulty we found a seat for Papa. He sat down in stony silence, and I realized that our life was in my hands. I ran around trying to find out what was going on and to get seats for the next flight. I knew some people at the airport from the days when I worked in the tourist business. It was hopeless. There were no flights. Another mystery, for the weather was good. By evening we saw that we wouldn't be leaving that day. Papa silently followed me to the bus back to town. We spent the night with friends since we couldn't get a hotel room. In the morning Papa sat grimly on a bench at the airport, refusing to eat. There was one plane, but it was a special flight—that is, for various bureaucrats. But by evening there was an avalanche of planes one after another. Where did they come from?

At midnight we were in a plane, and a shadow of a smile crossed Papa's pale face. Our torment was coming to an end.

We arrived very late at night and spent an hour waiting for our luggage. Father was melting. Dropping his usual caution and self-control, he along with a pleasant-looking Armenian cursed Soviet power. When Papa walked away, his new "friend" tried to make a date with me for the next day. All I was interested in was getting home. I had to keep Papa in a good mood to the end. We went out onto the square. It was empty, and the rare bus or taxi was immediately assailed by the furious crowd. We found a private car to take us for an enormous sum. We drove home along the empty, broad Moscow streets. Papa looked out the window and said pacifically, "It's so beautiful in Moscow. There's no better city as far as I'm concerned." He was calm and happy.

FEBRUARY 1. Trips abroad were even more dramatic. There was always uncertainty until the last moment. You could feel confident only when you had the passport and visa, foreign money, and the plane ticket in your pocket. But once even that wasn't enough.

Father was going with a delegation to an international congress in Tokyo. At the last moment the delegates learned that the trip's organizers had not ordered the tickets in time, so that they all had open tickets on the day of departure, without guaranteed seats. "If you can find yourself a seat, you go. If not, you have to turn in your passport and money within two days," said the "helpful" girls in the foreign travel department. You can imagine the state of a Soviet citizen who may be losing his only chance to see exotic Japan through the lapses of the Soviet bureaucratic system.

The families of all the delegates were at the airport first thing in the morning. There was only one flight that day, a stopover in Moscow. All our hopes were pinned on passengers who would get out in Moscow. We took up positions at all the registration counters just in case. You never know where anything will happen. Using my connections, I ran from counter to counter, scouting. Mama with her energy even managed to cross customs a few times by accident. We kept Papa out of this because the tension was unbearable. He still had a long trip ahead of him, a serious scientific report to make, and tiring days. We could rest up after he had left.

At last around four o'clock, the plane arrived and the truly dramatic moment had come: Would there be seats? My people whispered yes. The scientists, unable to believe their luck, registered their tickets, went through customs, and vanished beyond passport control. The families stood downstairs, practically weeping in relief. We decided to wait until the plane took off. And how right we were. About ten minutes later four of the eight delegates came back down the stairs with their briefcases— back from beyond the border. With his bad luck, Papa was one of them. They looked as if they had been sentenced to hard labor. They told us that at the last minute some Chinese or Koreans showed up with tickets for that flight.

On the way home Papa smiled crookedly and said that it could have been worse. We could see how upset he was. After all, he had anticipated this trip for months, had bought loads of books about Japan, and, with his intellectual curiosity, had memorized the country's geography. He didn't sleep that night.

The next morning was déjà vu: the same counters, the same stopover flight. We were afraid to believe in success. The remaining delegates got seats and disappeared beyond passport control. Papa was pale and stumbled as he walked away. We didn't go home until the plane was in the air.

That evening Papa's brother called. His voice resembles Papa's. At first I shuddered. *I saw the plane take off with my own eyes. Did they have a forced landing in Siberia, and he's being sent back?* My feverish imagination was working overtime. But I quickly realized that it was my uncle.

Each time we left for the airport we all sat down for a minute and wished Papa a bon voyage. It must have helped; he did go.

FEBRUARY 3.   Even though we had a car, we never traveled more than two or three hundred kilometers outside Moscow. The horror stories our friends told us were enough: trouble with gasoline, no food to be bought, no place to sleep. And God forbid the car break down. You could be stuck in some hole for several weeks. Once I had a marvelous incident with fuel right in the middle of Moscow. I was working with a group of American tourists who had come from Europe in a West German bus. We were running out of diesel fuel, and we were supposed to go to the theater that evening. Around three in the afternoon the driver and I went off in search of diesel fuel. We visited almost all the gas stations, but they were all out. We decided to go back to the hotel, pick up the tourists, dressed for the theater, and try once more. We got to a gas station, where a grim attendant came out and said that he had diesel fuel but the pump wasn't working. I begged him to do something. He came out with a huge hammer and began banging away at the pump with all his might. The diesel fuel didn't flow, I was on the verge of tears, and we were going to be late for the theater.

"Don't be upset," my tourists said. "We'll have other nights at the theater, but we'll never see a show like this again."

We went on in search of gas. After a few more kilometers we reached another station. We were outside town by now. A group of curious men, colorful and motley, one with a funny red cap on his head, came out to meet us. The diesel fuel poured into the tank. "Red Cap" was particularly helpful. The driver, with German precision, counted out the correct number of coupons for the fuel.

"No money, no coupons," the workmen said. "This is a

rich country; we can fill up more than one bus. Come back tomorrow; we'll give you as much as you need."

The Americans didn't understand what was happening, so I translated for them. The German was also surprised. Here we had spent half the day looking for diesel fuel, and now they were giving us liters of it for free. The tourists started collecting presents. They sent me to Red Cap and the others with panty hose and other foreign trifles. "Senkyew, senkyew," the men said.

There was something hurtful, touching, and sad about that event. The men at the station looked like friendly Russian fools before the tourists. Our truly rich country put people in ridiculous situations.

FEBRUARY 6. This morning I went to meet friends from Berlin at the train station, the famous Byelorussian station, from which trains left for the front in the early days of World War II. Now it is the window to Europe: Moscow–Berlin, Moscow–Paris, Moscow–Hanover. I think that of all the Moscow train stations it is the most peaceful and civilized. The Leningrad station is fairly decent, too.

Train stations have always played a special role in Russian life. A person of certain means could travel in comfort, style, and taste. The smallest stations had restaurants and bars. Gentlemen came out of the cars with their walking sticks, headed for the bar, had a shot of vodka and a sturgeon sandwich. The steam whistle blew, and they hurried back to their comfortable, warm compartments. Winter voyages were wonderful. Outside the window were snowy fields and forests, and you sat in warmth, drinking hot tea with lemon and conversing unhurriedly with your companions.

Even now train travel retains its fabled charm if you are traveling in a normal train and a good car. Once we couldn't get tickets for a compartment car and had to ride in the so-called common car. It was a nightmare. The lights were on overhead, the door to the next car banged all night, and there were drafts everywhere. Three hours before we reached Moscow, the conductor yelled, "Reveille!" like in the army. He had to collect the linen. With inviolable Soviet passivity the passengers got up as one, and five minutes later the car was a seething beehive—people removing and rebundling their sheets, lining up for the toilet, gathering their luggage. Then we spent another two and a half hours trying to get comfortable on the bare hard bunks to nap some more. I was boiling with anger at Soviet rule and our herdlike instincts.

But traveling in what's called a soft car is sheer pleasure. You can sleep until the last moment; no one bothers you. In the evening the waiter comes for your order for dinner with champagne, and the conductors are infinitely polite.

Now back to stations. In modern Soviet times they have turned into something colorful and awful. They have become places for people to sleep through the night, to drink, to whore—the pits. Unfortunate passengers spend days and nights waiting for trains here, and the lucky ones can sit on benches. The others have to sit on the floor. They eat in their spots, often on a spread-out newspaper, and change their babies there, too.

The train station has its own life day and night. Many of

its inhabitants are homeless, and this is their permanent refuge. There are also professional thieves, who prey on careless tourists. For very moderate prices you can get any pleasure you seek, although you may pay dearly afterward. I have friends who live not far from three stations, and half their building is occupied by station prostitutes.

A new feature of the stations under *perestroika* is a number of cooperative establishments. Now you can get a decent, albeit expensive meal. A crazy friend of mine, Lisa, went to work for a co-op at a station, selling meat patties at night. Now that's a school of life! She's a kind girl, and soon all the local bums and thieves became her friends and protectors. Uncle Grisha was a colorful character, a little old man of fifty or so who swept the floors. One night he showed up in a pair of glasses without lenses. Someone asked him why he was wearing the frames. He answered with complete seriousness, "My vision's getting worse with age."

The most interesting thing happened to Lisa a month ago. Some sailors came around at two in the morning and said that they were coming home from a foreign voyage. They had spent all their money and wanted to sell imported cosmetics immediately. Naturally Lisa's eyes lit up. She didn't have any money with her, so she called a friend who lived nearby. The friend agreed to have Lisa and the sailors come to her house ten minutes later. Lisa took some pals, the local thieves, with her for protection. They went to the friend's house, the girls bought a few cosmetics, and the group went back to the station. The sailors had lots of things, and their bags were still full of foreign stuff. They went to the toilet with the thieves, whom they now considered Lisa's honest and kind friends. They entrusted one of them, Petya, with their bags and went into the stalls. As Petya later told Lisa, he suffered through the greatest temptation of his life. Every day he risked being caught stealing a crummy five or ten rubles, and here he had thousands in his hands. All he had to do was slip out the door and get lost in the crowds. He'd become a millionaire by local standards. But his code of honor wouldn't let him. He was Lisa's friend and protector. How could he let her down? His legs were itching to go out the door, but some invisible force kept him in place. Petya told Lisa that he couldn't bear to be tempted like that again, and she should never put him in such a situation.

Occasionally I wander through railroad stations, immersing myself in that strange and fortunately unknown life. I like the smells and sounds of train platforms. But the truly incomparable sensation occurs while you wait for loved ones on the platform. The announcement comes: "Train number forty on track two." First the train's head slowly floats in, and then the cars crawl past, and you quickly calculate where the car you want will be and run down the platform. In the window you see dear, happy faces. That's where there is a mysterious abundance of life and emotion—beloved faces in a train window.

FEBRUARY 8. I didn't notice that more than a month has passed since the New Year. It was always my favorite holiday, but every year it gets sadder. I've stopped writing my wishes on a piece of paper. I've given up hope of meeting "him." In the last few years on December 31 I've wanted to hide far from my own life and its disappointments. How I'd love to get on a train and go to Berlin to see my dearest friends. Dreamer! What about the passport from OVIR (the Office of Visas and Registration) and the train ticket that has to be bought a month in advance? No, the best place is bed, where you can cuddle up under the blanket and dream about Paris, Berlin, the moon, and Venus.

Lately I've enjoyed lying in bed and recalling my travels, meetings with friends, marvelous friendly parties. My travels have given me many kind friends, some of whom have become part of my life.

The first time I went to Berlin I was in the middle of my divorce. We had made the decision and separated, but all the paper work lay ahead, and his things were still in my apartment.

It so happened in Berlin that I was living alone in an old, tiny apartment in the middle of town. In order to get to the entrance, I had to go under a dark, deep arch and then across a small tree-filled yard. During the day I walked around town, went to the museums and stores, and sat in cafés, but I'd hurry home before dark because I was afraid to come home late. The apartment was dark and gloomy, without a TV or a telephone. When the neighbors went up the stairs, the wooden treads creaked loudly, making me jump. I thought about Russian émigrés in Berlin after the Revolution who had lived in houses like this. In the evenings I opened the window and looked in the neighbors' windows in hope of seeing life and movement. It was quiet almost everywhere, the windows shut with thick curtains. I felt a bit like a prisoner. Old Berlin gave me a sense of the traditional German way of life.

One fine day my life changed magically. My friend, the owner of the apartment, was living somewhere else, but he dropped by to pick up things. I came home to find not only

Herbert but a stranger, who was smoking in the room. Herbert introduced us. Werner spoke excellent English, and he had just come back from Georgia with his son. He had brought a letter to Herbert from Georgian friends. He had never met Herbert before. We found a lot to talk about: the trip to Georgia, my impressions of Germany. Before leaving, Werner invited me to his house the next day.

I found myself with a marvelous, hospitable German family, and by the end of the evening we had become friends. In addition to everything else, we were united by our suffering in the socialist paradise. I told them about our problems, about the hopes and fears of our people. Werner exclaimed, "It's just the same here. So similar." I countered, "It's better here. At least you have food, clothing, and comfort." Our conversations went on all night.

Two days later I moved into my new friends' house. I lay in my cozy room and wept tears of joy. God had sent me so much understanding, love, and warmth in this home. Werner's wife, Renata, struggled with English, but we understood each other without words. Sometimes instead of "I am happy" she would say, "I am afraid." Once, as we were heading into town, Renata said, "Go get undressed." I asked if we were planning to go to a nudist camp. Their son, Stefan, spoke flawless English, and we told each other jokes. For example, a policeman with a book under his arm meets another policeman. "What's the book about?"

"It's very interesting; it's called logic. I'll explain it. For instance, do you have an aquarium?"

"Yes," replies his interested colleague.

"Then you like animals, and if you like animals, you must like people, and that means you must have a wife."

"Yes, of course, I have a wife."

"And if you have a wife, then you're not a homosexual."

"Amazing," the policeman says. "I think I'll buy that book."

An hour later he's walking down the street with his book and runs into yet another policeman, who asks about the book.

"It's a wonderful and useful book. I'll explain it to you. Do you have an aquarium?"

"No," replies his friend.

"Then you're homosexual," the enlightened policeman declares.

For some reason in East Germany police are the butt of jokes.

I left Germany feeling that I was leaving home. I stood in the train and wept inconsolably. My new friends reached through the window, trying to comfort me and talking of our next meeting. A year later I was back in Berlin.

FEBRUARY 10.   A real winter day: frost, bright sunshine, and clear, clean air. Ideal weather for cross-country skiing. I dressed warmly and headed for the nearest woods. I'm enchanted by the winter forest: snow-covered trees, ringing silence, air redolent of pine. I stopped every now and then, dissolving in the peace and quiet. It is always warmer in the woods, even on cold days; the wind doesn't penetrate here, and the pleasant rhythm of sliding warms me, too. I feel absolutely happy, and the noisy urban life seems ugly and meaningless at moments like this.

It got dark early, and it was time to go back. The quick run through a field on the way back reminded me of the treachery of Russian winters. A cold wind blew into my face, and my hands felt icy even in warm mittens. It was blissful to be home in a hot shower. I was ravenous and ate whatever came to hand. I stretched out on the couch and thought: *Well, at least Soviet rule hasn't taken everything away from us.*

FEBRUARY 12. Today I signed up for ship tickets. If you don't think about summer vacation now, it will be too late. This is one of the features of our life: We buy boots in the summer and sandals in the winter.

Traveling on a ship is the best vacation for me. A ship is the best way to see the real Russia, vanishing into the past and desperately trying to survive, impoverished and infinitely rich spiritually, dear and unique. And the best way to travel is not on a special tour ship but on an ordinary route. It stops at small places where the tourists never go.

As soon as you get aboard, a measured life begins that is full of new experiences at the same time. You settle into a comfortable cabin (naturally, you must go first class) and run to take a spot in the restaurant. You have to hurry; otherwise you end up on the second shift and will have to look at dirty dishes from the previous seating before you are served. Then you check out the decks and the passengers, looking for the more decent-looking faces; meeting new people is part of the vacation pleasures. Finally you settle in a deck chair, and the most charming part of the trip starts: looking at the shore, the villages and small towns floating by. It's amazing, you can sit for hours and never get tired.

Every day the ship stops for several hours, sometimes in big cities, sometimes in small godforsaken spots. You wander down unpaved streets, looking at old wooden houses, half-ruined churches, and ancient estates, and your heart winces with love and sadness. What is happening to this great, beautiful country? What curse has befallen it, and for what sins? Russia could be one of the richest countries in the world, but its people are struggling for simple survival.

One of the most horrible aspects of provincial life is drunkenness. People drink from depression, from frustration, and simply out of habit. They drink everything that comes to hand: vodka, wine, moonshine, lab alcohol, lotions, and colognes. I was told about a small town in Siberia where almost all the men had blue faces. The local factory manufactured some kind of technical liquid that was blue and contained alcohol, so they all drank it instead of vodka.

Against this background of total blackout, you have the lovely regional museums with old furniture, paintings, and stories of the local guides about the former cultural life of these cities, about the famous writers and artists who visited. In places like that you can find pure people, who have managed to preserve islands of spirituality in this hopeless atmosphere. These people have marvelous libraries at home since there is a lot of time for reading on the long nights and there's no place to go anyway. Thanks to these people, tiny threads of Russian culture still extend throughout the land.

It is amusing to see advertisements for American films, local rock groups, punks, and other imitations of Western fashions. It's a funny, ridiculous parody at times. America seems as far away as the moon or Mars. But what can you do? Young people want to live in the twentieth century. They just don't know how to adjust to it. There used to be a joke about modern times. Japanese specialists come to the Soviet Union. They inspect a factory and say, "We thought that it would take you twenty years to catch up to us, but it turns out you'll be behind forever."

Yes, the Russian provinces live in their own dimension, often contrary to common sense but with mystical attraction and enigmatic power.

I've wandered very far from the ship. It's time to get back on deck. There's not a lot of space on a ship, so in a day or two everyone knows everyone else by sight, and there are all kinds of gossip and squabbles—someone is talking too loudly under a window, someone has a repulsive face. That adds variety to the trip, too, but on the whole, people are in good spirits, and the ship's steady motion and the changing views have a wonderful effect on the nervous system.

The big Volga ships take a lot of transient passengers. This is often a sad sight. They don't have berths booked, and they sleep in the corridors. Many carry lots of luggage, sacks, and bags. They have to be alert at night, so that their things aren't stolen. These people are used to hard lives, they've never seen any other, so they don't complain. I remember a toothless old man with a peg leg, who slept outside the door of our cabin one night. I felt awful, but what could we have done? In the morning he was in a good mood and joked around as he loaded up the heavy sacks on his back. To a girl who had grown up in a modern Moscow apartment, this life seemed scary and hard to understand. But that's exactly how a great part of the country lived.

I also remember Gypsies at the Nizhnevolzhsky landing. I've never seen others like them. They were real, free Gypsies of the steppe. The men were tall and handsome with tar black hair and piercing blue eyes. They wore red shirts and wide trousers. The women and children huddled behind them. The Gypsies casually leaned on the railing and studied us. We were exotic for them, too. I thought the handsome men had come out of the pages of nineteenth-century novels. Russian gentlemen might catch a glimpse of Gypsies, get off the ship, and run off to sprees and to burn away their lives. "I'll go off with a crowd of Gypsies, they know how not to mourn," claimed a popular song back then.

These voyages by ship allowed me to learn about and love the real Russia. Only now, many years later, do I fully realize that.

FEBRUARY 15. I haven't written for several days. There was a lot to do at work. I've reread what I have written so far and have decided that I have to write some more about one of my trips to the heart of Russia.

One day I decided that I was tired of civilized vacations and I headed out into the countryside. Friends arranged a trip to a tourist base on Lake Seliger. It's not that far, an overnight trip by train, but it's very remote and beautiful.

Mama, our friend, and I arrived early in the morning. An

ugly modern building stood on the lake, and it made me feel a little sad. The room was ascetically gloomy and cold, the floor in the bathroom was raw concrete, the sink and toilet were dirty and broken, and none of the electric outlets worked. We cheered ourselves up by saying we had come for the fresh air and we'd only be sleeping in the room. We went to breakfast. It was a huge room of dubious cleanliness, and like most such places, it lacked knives. The food was barely edible. We gave ourselves another counseling session and decided to get on with the vacation immediately.

We went for a walk. The locale was divine: an ancient church on a hill, an abandoned small cemetery, the lake stretching into infinity, and half-ruined village houses. We wandered around half the day and returned to so-called civilization. Pop music blared, men were walking around in jogging suits, and the hotel stank of cheap cafeteria food. Dinner consisted of hamburgers made with spoiled meat, and despite my nonfinickiness, I couldn't eat.

We put up with the joys of the tourist life for three days and then admitted we had to get out of there. We signed up for a week-long canoe trip. At least we'd be out of the hotel, and we'd do our own cooking over a fire and be in the middle of the countryside.

A group of fifteen people got together. We loaded up the boats and cast off. About three hours later we came across a miraculous sight: a large monastery on an island in the middle of the Seliger lake. It had been founded several centuries ago and was famous all over Russia. From afar it looked like a piece of St. Petersburg: granite banks, a large cathedral with several cupolas in the center, and numerous church buildings. Pilgrims—noblemen and simple folk—traveled to the site and lived here for weeks at a time, for the monastery received and fed everyone. While the monastery looked majestic and beautiful from afar, up close it was a pitiful sight. In the early years of Soviet rule almost all the priests were shot or sent to labor camps. The churches and cathedrals were shut and turned into warehouses. The other buildings were used to house invalids. Later a penal colony for minors was set up on the island. One of the punishments was forcing the boys up a scaffolding high in a cupola to chip away chunks of the ancient frescoes. What a fine way to instill love for Russian culture! They also broke off pieces of stone and brick from the old buildings to use in local construction. Gradually everything fell into total disrepair, and the monastery cells were turned into grim skeletons of once-lovely abodes. The local guides told us about all this with pain and hopelessness. They said that restoration had been under way for many years, but there was almost no money, and the needed repairs would take several decades. We saw no more than three or four workmen on the entire territory, but the local tourist base was doing good business. It was handing out boats, sleeping bags, and canned goods. The tourist camp workers told us proudly that there was a plan to turn the entire island into a major tourist complex. "Once we restore the monastery buildings, we'll turn them into hotels, open a museum in the main cathedral, and this place will be civilized at last." It didn't occur to any of them to return the monastery to the Russian Orthodox Church and to restore its former glory.

As we rode away from the island, my head was spinning

with a banal truth: It is so hard to create and so easy to destroy. That island was a symbol of the mockery made of Russian culture and the Church.

We followed a narrow, brush-covered stream to a small inland lake, where we set up for our forest life. These were the best days of our vacation. We rose early, wandered in the woods, rowed around the lake. The discomforts spoiled things a bit. The tent was too small, we had to turn over together at night like prisoners on plank beds, the mosquitoes were vicious, and there was nowhere to wash up because the lake was too cold for swimming. For two days I didn't undress or change; then I got sick of feeling like a filthy animal. I went into the bushes with a bucket of warm water, stripped, and had a forest wash. It was so good!

As in any Soviet collective, the squabbling and gossip started in a couple of days: Someone was skipping out on chores, someone else was eating too much, and so on. Against the harmony and majesty of nature, people seemed silly and incongruous. I tried to participate as little as possible in this "Soviet life."

On the way back there was a strong wind, the boat was in turbulent waves, and it was scary. I felt seasick for several hours after we landed. For me, an urban resident, the trip was like a frontier expedition. I felt strong and hardened by life and regarded my calluses proudly.

We were given a present in farewell: We were taken to the neighboring tourist camp. It was another sad and depressing sight. It was situated in a dilapidated estate. The once-large and luxurious ballrooms and halls were broken up into tiny rooms without toilets or sinks. It rained that day, muddy goo squished underfoot, and the vacationers stared out sadly at the world from the windows of their little cells. I was ready to go home to Moscow.

Oh, I forgot to mention that our tourist base was described in an article in *National Geographic*. The former director created a luxurious Western-style life for himself on company funds. He bought foreign stereos and TV, drove a fancy car, and lived it up at the best Black Sea resorts. I hear he was arrested. The new director, it was said, was a fine and honest man. But then why were the vacationers still fed rotten meat when they had paid so much for their stay?

On the way back in the train I had already forgotten the unpleasant parts, and all that remained were memories of a fairy-tale lake, the silence, the forest smells, the dawns and sunsets, the old church on a hill. We promised one another to come back the following year, but to head straight for the woods on the lake, skipping the tourist base. As it turned out, I was in Germany the following summer.

CHAPTER EIGHT

More Miscellany

FEBRUARY 19. It's incredible what's happening with Soviet power! Where's class hatred?

It's all these Petersburg things. As a late elderly woman used to say to her son-in-law when he did something unusual by her standards, "It's that drop of noble blood in you acting up." Incidentally, there was more than a drop in him; a good half was noble Russian and English blood.

Leningrad TV news showed a charming descendant of the Volkonsky family. She lives, as most Russian aristocratic émigrés do, in Paris, and came to see the homeland of her ancestors. She spoke Russian beautifully. The reporter's commentary was completely unexpected: "Look at the refined face and manners of this young woman. She represents generations of the Russian aristocracy." The aristocracy that they had cruelly and thoroughly exterminated since the first days of the Revolution. Now, suddenly, they are coming to their senses. They understand at last that the aristocrats were not the idle bloodsuckers who were robbing Russia. They were first of all people, among whom were both scoundrels and upstanding citizens, useless individuals and geniuses. The Russian aristocrats were always the bearers of the great Russian culture. And culture was not created during banquets and drinking sprees. The talented poet Vladimir Mayakovsky, confused by the Revolution, once wrote, "Eat pineapples and munch on pheasant, your final day is coming, bourgeois!" All schoolchildren in the Soviet Union know those lines. But do they also know that in aristocratic families children were brought up in harsh discipline and asceticism? They got up at six, washed in ice water, and started their lessons, which lasted for many hours a day. Pushkin's education at the lycée is the best example of aristocratic upbringing. And who, if not the aristocracy, demonstrated for the dignity and rights of everyone at Senate Square in 1825?

By the way, who more than the aristocracy knew how to stand up and mock its own weaknesses? The classic image of the noble loafer Oblomov was created by the Russian nobleman Ivan Goncharov.

I admit that I am not objective, for I, too, have that "drop of noble blood acting up." Peter the Great himself gave one of our ancestors a gift. But I lack the nobleman's upbringing, and I don't have the control, the patience, the profound Christian piety.

I always dreamed about living in the nineteenth century, on an estate with large grounds and a pond with lilies, going to the capital for the holidays, and bearing and bringing up young noblemen. My mother always replied to my dreams, "And what if you were born a peasant girl or a servant in a master's house?"

"That's impossible," I replied. "After all, I'm not dreaming of being born an empress, just an ordinary (hereditary?) noble."

Noble or not, I'm surely a fruitless dreamer.

FEBRUARY 22. I'm feeling sad and lonely. I want to fall in love, but with whom? In the West, it is said, there are clubs for singles, and even if you don't find someone, you'll chase away your glum thoughts. When Mama was young, she and her friends went to dances and met people that way. But where can you go now? To the House of Cinematographers, the House of Writers? When I was twenty, I loved those places. Famous actors and writers might gaze at you in a lazily interested way, and that was enough for rapturous gossip with my girl friend for weeks.

Once, out of great love for literature or for writers, we went for a vacation at the writers' resort. It was the "dead season," when writers prefer to be in town. But we were wildly popular among those present . . . as fellow drinkers. Writers like to talk when they're drinking, and what could be better than two young and pretty girls delighted by everything they say? It was very innocent, and nothing more was expected of us.

I admit that I fell in love with one of the writers anyway. In the evening, barefoot so that no one would hear, I crept to his room. We drank strong tea and kissed, nothing more.

Now I don't need adventures like that. I've outgrown them.

Even earlier, when I was fourteen, my cousin and I spent hours making up stories about affairs with movie stars. Her "beloved" was Marcello Mastroianni, and mine was Alain Delon. The basic story line was that they both would come with us to Kaluga, and we all would live with our grandparents. We had endless discussions of the sensation they would cause in our neighborhood. All the neighbors would come running while we stood there arm in arm with the handsome stars. We divided up the beds, who would sleep where. My cousin and Marcello, since she was older, got the big bed, and Alain and I the smaller one. I don't know what we intended to do with Grandmother and Grandfather since there were only two rooms. We talked about what Grandmother would feed them, what we would wear, whom we'd invite to dinner, and so on. No end of fantasies.

FEBRUARY 25. More about aristocrats. They were taught to keep diaries from childhood. It was supposed to train them in self-discipline, analysis, and evaluation of their actions. I can confirm that it's work that demands great willpower. So many ideas come into your head during the day, and mentally you write everything down. But there's a big difference between writing mentally and writing with a pen at the desk. You have to make special shackles to keep yourself at the desk for an hour or two every day. When I was a child, we had a maid who thought that every literate person could be a writer, as long as pen and paper were handy. Writing a dozen pages was like doing the laundry or washing the floor for her.

I had so many excuses for not sitting down to work. When I played the piano, I kept pestering my mother every five minutes: I needed a drink; I had to go pee. I processed a lot of water in thirty minutes. When I was writing my thesis, I reorganized the kitchen shelves and the closets and ironed a lot of clothes. When I was working on my dissertation, I kept American best sellers under my manuscripts. If Mama came into the room, I pretended to be really busy.

But as soon as I started, things went smoothly. Sometimes

you spend two hours in the torment of getting ready and then sit down and finish the work in an hour. Keeping this diary is both pleasure and torment for me.

MARCH 1. Last night I dreamed I was flying. You push off, make an effort, and you're soaring. An incredible sensation. Once I dreamed I was rushing at great speed through a tunnel. People say you see that during clinical death. I had been very upset that day and tried to find solace from my problems. Strange things also happen to me when I'm making love. I travel to other eras and see enormous buildings. My lover knocked himself out to please me, and I told him about a Gothic cathedral I saw. He was hurt. Silly man, it was much better than physical satisfaction. Another time there were Chinese dragons and fighting warriors in exotic garb.

I suppose the time has come for me to reveal my sweet secret about the island of Crete. About ten years ago I was on a cruise in the Mediterranean. I prepared for the trip well, read a lot of books about the countries we were going to visit. And suddenly there was an unexpected change in the route. Egypt was dropped, too unsettled, and we went to Crete. To my shame I knew almost nothing about it except that I confused it with Cyprus. We came ashore on a cool gray morning and saw the walls of the old city. We went by bus to the ruins of the palace of Knossos. The name meant almost nothing to me.

We arrived an hour later. There were ruins like any other, nothing special. I had seen similar ones in Central Asia and in Syria. We went through the wrecked rooms, up and down steps.

They say that déjà vu happens to people who are exhausted or emotionally stunned. I was calm and not in the least tired. I simply realized that I had lived here before. I had walked along these corridors, carrying water pitchers and speaking a different language. Alas, I had been a simple servant. Of course, it would have been better to be a noble lady, but you can't fool with your memory. Most important, I had been happy in that life. I had a lover with whom I went into the hills and swam in the sea. My desires had been simple and satisfiable. In a word, there had been harmony, which was so lacking from my present life. I wasn't inventing any fantasies. I just walked around and remembered.

In the afternoon we went to a museum that kept frescoes and utensils from the palace. More confirmation—I had seen them all before. Every line, every shade of color I recognized with my entire being.

That night on the ship I checked and rechecked my sensations. Had I invented it or had it happened? And what if my lover were alive once more, like me? And what if I met him again, since I'd never had such a joyous and natural love in my life yet? This was where the romantic dreams began.

I told my discovery to parapsychologist friends. They assured me that I had lived then and had also lived in ancient Egypt, where I had been a priestess in a temple. My boyfriend suggested that I not fill my head with nonsense and concentrate on ordinary love instead. But after my love in Knossos I didn't need him.

MARCH 3. In every Russian there lurks a bit of Oblomov. That famous hero of Russian literature spent most of his life in bed or in an armchair wearing his robe. His best intentions were shattered against his immovable indolence and inability to function.

Today I was a real Oblomov. I spent the day in my nightgown and robe, and naturally I didn't make my bed. But Moscow weather can make you do that sometimes! You open your curtains and see a dark, lowering sky and drizzling rain. You go to the bathroom to wash your face and get back into bed to read a bit. Then you pull on your robe and wander to the kitchen. Breakfast and a cup of tea wake you up a bit. You call a girl friend, talk for ten minutes, and then you want to get back into bed. The rain is coming down harder, and a cold wind is howling. The cozy bed in the corner with the soft light of the lamp above it is so inviting. There's a pile of books and magazines by the bed. You read for a half hour, and you're sleepy again. Sleeping in the daytime is very much like being half awake. It's incredibly delicious.

Then it's lunchtime. It might as well be twilight outside. You shut the kitchen curtains, turn on the table lamp, tune in to Radio Liberty, and it's like being in Europe. A friend of mine, when he opened the curtains in the morning, always said, "Well, is there still Soviet rule out there?" Lunch lasts almost an hour. Then you call your mother, who's also reading on the couch. Well, you might turn on the TV. I have it set up so that I can watch from bed. Back under the blanket, I'm getting completely lazy. What else do you need out of life? The evening flies by. If I can't control myself, I have something else to eat at bedtime. Then it's back to a book until sleep creeps up on me.

In this foul weather, to nature's dreary plaint,
Days, moments like years, years go slowly.

A lot of people in Moscow complain about the autumn and winter hibernation: You don't want to do anything, and you don't have the strength to go out. Of course, our hibernation is not seasonal. It's been going on for decades. Some sleep at work; some sleep at home. You have to agree that it's nicer at home.

MARCH 4. They made me cry today. I decided to go swimming at the pool on Sundays. With difficulty I managed to buy a pass for three months, which required a note from my doctor. I went to the hospital, which said I had to give samples for analysis and also go see the venerealogical service. It's protecting Soviet people from VD and other vile diseases. Why not a psychiatric check as well? What if you start attacking your sports companions? Well, I went to the service. I got lost and asked some old ladies in the courtyard for the right building. They gave me a dirty look and said nastily, "You need that yellow building. That's what you need." I was already on the verge of tears. The exam lasted one minute. I lifted up my blouse and lowered my panties. Everything was fine. There were no horrible ulcerations on my body from a corrupt life. A doctor at the hospital could have done the very same thing. But an easy life is a luxury in our country.

Tomorrow at seven I have to give blood and other specimens. I visualized the line in the stuffy hallway, the tales of the old women about diseases, and then another line for an hour and a half to see the doctor. I burst into tears and told my mother that I was giving up on the pool and would tear up my pass.

Mama didn't argue. She disappeared for an hour and returned with a note from her own doctor; as a war veteran she is able to go to a privileged hospital. We erased her name and wrote in mine. As wise people say, you have to think.

MARCH 7. We're trying to make up for lost time like mad. There's an explosion of intellectual and political life in Moscow, a steady stream of evenings with celebrities, literary evenings, exhibitions. *Samizdat* books, so recently banned, are read from the stage in large halls. New prose has come out from the underground. It ruthlessly strikes your psyche. Some people can't take it and start attaching labels as in the good old days: pornography, slander, exaggeration. One insulted listener got up at a literary evening and said she thought this was a public mockery of Soviet people.

And our life isn't a mockery? Wake up and open your eyes! Don't have the nerve?

It's not easy reading this prose. This isn't your socialist realism, where everything is beautiful, joyful, and understandable, where the world is black and white, the good guy always wins, the workers go on building developed socialism, the peasants grow a bountiful harvest, and the intellectuals, a mere substratum of society, help as best they can. Here you are inundated with drunkards, drug addicts, sexual maniacs, cynical, corrupt functionaries. Here you have vomit, bad smells, corpses, morbid fantasies, and degenerate children.

Sometimes this prose is presented in a complex, irrational form, but how else can you talk about our irrational, absurd reality?

Its most unexpected effect is healing. It's like an inoculation. You have a light form of the disease, and then the disease is no longer a threat.

This prose helped me in my difficult moments when my mind rejected what was happening. What could be more horrible than the death of someone you love? It turns out that even that can be made twice as bad. We took my father back to his hometown to be buried, and there wasn't a single morgue prepared to hold his coffin for one night. As a result, we left him in a small wooden building without refrigeration or air conditioning in ninety-degree heat. It was the morgue of the forensics lab. When the men came out of the building, having left the coffin in there, they stank with the horrible corpse smell. My cousin was as white as death. He said that there were three rotting corpses of a greenish blue color on the tables, and the floor was covered with a malodorous slime. The next day the coffin was permeated with that smell. I couldn't get rid of it for several months. I'd be walking down the street, and it would come upon me out of nowhere—the bushes, a doorway.

Tell me, why did my father have to spend his last night on earth in that hell?

Of course, he had seen that for himself a few years earlier. His brother died unexpectedly during a vacation in a famous resort city. According to Russian Orthodox tradition, the body must be buried, not cremated. It was important for Papa to have the whole family buried in one place. It took three weeks to transport the body five hundred miles. There was no coffin for transportation, and all the forms of transport refused to take the body. And there were worms and maggots all over the morgue; the only morgue in the city had no cooling system.

My father came home aged by several years.

So when I stood near the house with the bodies and listened to my cousin, I recalled those horror stories so that I could distance myself from the unbearable . . . and go on living.

In the first hours after my father's death I also had to deal with pathological cruelty. His was an almost instantaneous death, at home, over breakfast. We didn't want an autopsy. The cause of death was clear: He had a bad heart. We had to get a certificate from the hospital where he was treated. The doctor said with blatant nastiness, "If you're so Orthodox, then keep your relative at home until the funeral. They do autopsies on everyone at the morgue." It was hot, and the funeral was several days away. The doctors kept me in the hallways almost a half hour, walking past me, looking important. It was a form of sadistic pleasure for them. I couldn't take it. I called Mama and screamed so the whole hospital could hear, "These bitches won't give me the certificate." Everything was ready in ten minutes. They brought me a sedative and tried to calm me down. They had got what they wanted: They had humiliated me, and then they could take pity on me.

MARCH 10. I can't control myself, I'm still shaking. I have to buy a gun on the black market. I was coming back from friends' tonight, and I was rather well dressed, in a German fur jacket. A suspicious-looking young man sat in the bus across from me. His head was lowered, and half his face was covered by his collar. When I got off, he followed at a distance. Then he took another path and met me near the entrance. The street was empty. In the small entry you have to punch in a code to open the inner door. He was waiting for me to enter the code. I jumped out into the street. Luckily a young man of eighteen or so was walking by. I said, "Help me, some strange guy is following me." The guy was pushing all the buttons, trying to hit on the code. It was after midnight. Nobody goes visiting at that hour. I opened the door, and the guy followed us to the elevators. We stopped and waited to see what would happen. He got into an elevator, the door shut, and the lights went up to the seventh floor and then back down. Our elevators don't return automatically. That meant he was still in it. We got on the other elevator and went up to my floor. I asked the young man if he was afraid to go back down. He laughed and said of course not.

Am I crazy? Obviously he had been following me. I don't even want to think what he wanted: the jacket, my jewelry, or me? There is a dark stairway by the elevator which no one uses. He could have dragged me in there and done whatever he wanted.

A terrible crime wave has hit the country. Just a few years ago I often came home at one or two in the morning. I would walk from the bus stop down paths through thick brush and never worry. Now we try not to go out after six in the evening. The crimes are of all kinds, from mugging to vicious rapes and murders. There have been incidents in our building, some with comic overtones. A famous speculator in Western electronic equipment lives across the way. It is said that people shot into his windows from the house across the street. And the former chairman of our building cooperative, a physics teacher, recently robbed his next-door neighbor. The dog followed the scent to his apartment, which was full of the neighbors' things. They didn't take him to court. They settled amicably.

Now you can be robbed in the metro. Gangs surround you and, knives in hand, politely ask you to take off your jewelry and clothes. Some even take your shoes and give you a pair of house slippers. These gangs are called Slippers.

It's a good thing that I had military training at college. I know the strategy and tactics of battle, and I know how to do reconnaissance. When I leave the apartment, I reconnoiter the area. Anyone in the hallway or behind the garbage dump? If there's a man in the elevator, I wait for the next one. Once I practically pushed a man out who was getting on. And I'm alert all the time—on the street, the trolley, the metro. Battle-ready. All I need is a gun.

MARCH 15. Was this really the last time? I came home, washed, warmed up, had some hot tea, and felt like a human being. The worst part of it all is its meaninglessness and humiliation. It's been going on for almost twenty years, since my school days. It's called helping your hometown. Everyone, from schoolchildren to Ph.D.'s, works at the vegetable warehouse every two or three months, supposedly to help save the harvest that the workers there are artfully letting rot. Naturally we don't go in to work that day, but we get our usual salaries. So I guess it costs the state a lot to have a professor rummaging around in the rotting potatoes. There was a joke in a movie I saw: A Ph.D. put his card into every sack of potatoes he handled, so the customer would know who had done this highly specialized task.

The workers at the vegetable warehouse consider us slaves and never miss an opportunity to show their power: We'll let you go home when we feel like it; if you don't work well, we'll tell your boss. And they hang around doing nothing. The worst is always the director of the warehouse. Usually it's a fat peroxide blonde with teased hair and many diamond rings. She comes to work in her own car or the business Volga. She's full of majesty and self-love. Of course, these ladies lead a hard life. It's not easy making all the deals they do, and they could end up in jail. But according to the saying, no risk, no champagne.

Today was like every other time. We came at eight and hung around for a half hour, waiting for our assignments. Finally we were told to chop cabbage for sauerkraut. The workers gave us big knives, dirty aprons, and whisk brooms and showed us to our workplace, outside under a canopy. There was a cold drizzle, and our hands froze in the wet gloves. We chopped cabbage on the tables and tossed it onto a moving conveyor belt. Then it was allegedly washed and placed into large urns for pickling; these were underground, with the openings at floor level covered with wooden boards. Workers walk over them from time to time in their dirty boots. It helps pack the cabbage down. They say the fermentation kills bacteria, but I'm not going to buy sauerkraut anymore. By one o'clock I had started to go crazy. My hands and feet were freezing, and I needed to go to the toilet. But the toilets here are so bad that you have to shut your eyes and hold your breath, so it's better to wait until you get home. We started winding up around two, cleaning off the tables, sweeping the floor. At two-thirty we went to the exit, showed our bags (to prove we weren't hiding a head of cabbage worth seven kopecks), and headed for the bus. I sat in a corner on the way home, trying to warm up and thinking how lucky I was. I was going home to my own apartment with a hot shower, food, and comfortable bed. But a few decades ago women like me worked twelve-hour days in minus-forty-degree weather, went home to damp filthy barracks, ate disgusting gruel, and slept under rags. I am truly lucky not to have been born in Stalinist times.

MARCH 20. Today I watched a Soviet movie from the thirties on TV. The movies made in those terrible years are so full of charming simplicity and marvelous lies. The Stalinist era created an attractive myth. It took hold in all art forms—literature, film, painting, architecture. A whole system of archetypes was created: the hero, the villain, the good and bad women, the typical conflict situation, and so on. The system became so developed over the years that the good guys all combed their hair the same way, had the same smile, and used the same expression, while the bad guys were all alike, too. If you were to feed everything into a computer, you could produce the model novel of the Stalinist era.

The most amazing thing is that the signs of those times

have a magical effect on me. It may be due to my childish recollections of the fifties. When we would come from a party late at night, I often would lie on the backseat of the car and look up at the heavy, clumsy Stalinist buildings. They represented the protection of my happy way of life as a child; after all, we had also lived in a communal flat of the late forties. I liked the exquisitely tasteless statues of Pioneers, phys ed majors with oars in their hands, and the young naturalists. It was reliable and uncomplicated. There were marvelous songs on the radio. "I know of no other country where a man can breathe this free" or "Oh, it's so good living in the Soviet land, so good!" There was a joke about that song in the seventies: An inspection commission came to a mental home. A patient chorus was enthusiastically singing the song. One patient was silent. The commission asked why. "He's almost cured," the doctor replied.

I have to give this era its due: It has stayed on in my memory as a time of abundance. The big stores in the middle of town displayed huge hams, various kinds of sturgeon and salmon, black and red caviar. Jewelry stores had unique antique diamonds, and the fur sections of department stores had luxurious fur coats and fur collars of all kinds. We couldn't afford any of it, but it was there. My parents occasionally splurged on caviar since it was supposed to be very healthy for children.

I know what the times were really like, and my emotional attachment to them is more of a nostalgic whim. But there are still many people who believe the myth and mourn the lost grandeur of the Stalinist superpower.

MARCH 25. My work was always in the category "Fighter on the ideological front." A fine fighter I was, my head stuffed with Voice of America, Radio Liberty, and other Western news services. At least I knew "the enemy's face" well. Sometimes the enemy seemed so attractive I wanted to hurry into battle . . . and give myself up.

But we were supposed to fight the "false propaganda" of the Western way of life—that is, prove that a crowded trolley was much more comfortable than some Cadillac because our medical care was free or that a vacation at a dirty tourist base was better than a trip to Hawaii because we had free education. We followed the principle expressed in the song "At least we're making missiles, covering the Yenisey River, and even in the sphere of ballet we're ahead of the rest of the planet."

We had to cover up the "small drawbacks" of our society (that's our historical burden!). If you were in a restaurant with foreigners and a cockroach was swimming in your cup, you had to swallow it so that the ideological foes wouldn't see it. If the roach was in a foreigner's cup, you had to hypnotize him (the foreigner, not the roach) and tell him that it was an unground coffee bean. If the water was turned off at the hotel during a heat wave, you had to think of some huge accident in America that would make this incident seem like a trifle. You needed incredible erudition and extraordinarily quick thinking.

Also, you had to appear to be the model Soviet person— happy, businesslike, and of high morals. You had to have on hand a story about your cloudless family happiness, your healthy Pioneer children and Komsomol brothers. And God forbid you should ever fall for the charms of a foreigner. The ideological foe had to be a sexless and unattractive creature for you. And if you felt the slightest hint of weakness, you had to run for the hills.

But the ranks of fighters thinned. The "fallen" girls came back after a while to visit their parents, looking prettier and happier. This raised some doubts with the rest.

Of course, it's easy to write about this now with light irony. Luckily the "ideological front" is gradually falling apart. But just a few years ago there was real paranoia. Incidentally, for the sake of justice, it is said that Americans had similar feelings about us. I find it hard to believe.

MARCH 28. The eternal argument: spiritual Russia and unspiritual West. My artist friend recently said, "We are so devilishly spiritual because we don't have anything else." I'm not prepared to discuss this issue on a global level, but I think that there is something hysterical in our spirituality, especially lately. We like to read about tragic fates, travel back mentally to the horrible Stalinist times, and talk about the end of the world. I think this is some form of penance for our sins. We must go through the bloody horrors once more, mentally, before moving on. But it's turning into an unhealthy situation; we're stuck in the moment of redemption. As Bulat Okudjava says in his song, "Don't make an idol for yourselves out of the sins of our eternal Russia." Of course, that's in the Russian character, too: We like to pick at our wounds. We keep upsetting ourselves and being under stress.

There are so few simple pleasures in our daily lives that we unwittingly seek substitutes. In other words, we are trying to replace our joyless real life with the world of thoughts, ideas, and vicarious emotions. Long ago I thought, *I've lived through so many other people's lives in books that I haven't had time to live my own.*

But who knows what's better, our pleasure "on the edge" or a steady and boring satisfaction? Probably the golden mean is best, but where do you find it?

MARCH 30. There's a lot of talk about national or ethnic problems. People used to say that we were a special creation of Mother Nature, a single Soviet people. When that one nation began killing one another in the Caucasus, people remembered that there are different nationalities, religions, and roots. Having decided that we are all the same, we lost respect for our own characteristics and traditions and for those of others. We rejected ourselves.

I have a strange attitude toward my nationality. I always wanted to have national feelings. I envied the smaller nationality groups who had retained them. My Armenian, Georgian, and Estonian friends were the best examples of that. The Soviet rule seems to have finished off the Russians forever, replacing us with Soviets. For foreigners, "Russian" and "Soviet" became synonyms. For the other ethnic groups living in our country, we turned into oppressors. I've traveled a lot around the country and heard unkind things about Russians. I began to wonder why.

Instead of national pride I developed something akin to shame and a sense of being cheated. When conversation turned to nationalities, I would talk about the benefits of cosmopolitanism. I'd say I was Russian almost apologetically. I thought that everything really Russian perished in 1917. This is partially true because at that time Russian culture suffered a terrible blow and later Stalin destroyed its greatest bearers.

At the same time I was given a very Russian upbringing. My grandfather taught me to love the Russian countryside with a special feeling. Papa read Pushkin to me when I was little, and we'd lie on the couch and listen to Tchaikovsky's *Seasons*. As a history teacher Mama told me a lot about Russia's olden days. I knew many poems by Russian poets by heart. But I also heard a lot at home about the crimes committed by the Russian people or in the name of the Russian people. I think that my parents were both proud and ashamed of being Russian.

Now I write about these mixed feelings in the past tense. Our national penance is helping us overcome the shame. The words "I'm Russian" no longer stick in my throat. But at the same time I very much dislike the extremes some Russians are falling into, blaming their woes on other nations. If you allowed something to be done to you, that means you're weak, and it's your own fault. Instead of looking for whom to blame, you'd be better off restoring your dignity, so that you will be respected once again. There is much for which Russians could be esteemed.

APRIL 2. My friend Nadya and I took a trip for a few days to the small Russian town of Podolsk, where her grandmother's old house is. Nothing compares with these provincial towns.

They're where the true Russian spirit lives. These places used to be cultural centers, where famous writers and artists summered, but now they're just dilapidated provinces. Their old wooden house stands at the edge of town, with a dreary empty lot beyond it, and farther down that road is an old monastery in ruins, called Vysoky. You can see it from the living room. The air there is filled with tranquillity and a mix of charm and sorrow. The house is big, with several rooms, a kitchen, and wide terrace. The old heavy furniture, the stove, and a wall clock with a melodic ring and a pendulum survived. A big hare named Nura and two dogs, one old and silly, the other young and pushy, play in the yard.

We took a walk in the daytime. We went to the old bazaar, which sells everything from hamsters, birds, and nanny goats to very scholarly tomes. The books cost more than the goats. The local museum exhibits objects from the town's aristocratic past—paintings, tables, curtains, dishes. But the modern stores are empty, as if the town lived only in the past. The present looks grim. There was one long line in town—for vodka. It's a good system. The buyer thrusts his hand with a ten-ruble note in it through a small window and pulls it out holding a bottle of vodka. We stood and watched for a long time. The impression was that of a robot working smoothly inside the window. It was rhythmic and perfect. Then we went into a church turned into a museum, housing a show of local artists. It was amusing to see surrealist paintings, in the style of a provincial Russian Dali, hanging in this old Russian building. The door was open, and a goat came in to eat the flowers from a vase. The custodian yelled at the goat and tried to chase it out, but it stubbornly refused to budge, bleating loudly. Everyone laughed, and I think the people were on the goat's side.

The trip took me back to my Kaluga childhood. I felt good but sad. Coming back to Moscow was like entering another world.

APRIL 3. My adventure with the suspicious-looking guy was nothing compared with a truly mysterious and perhaps even tragic incident. Friends of mine cannot find their daughter, a beautiful eighteen-year-old brunette. She recently married, and she and her husband decided to spend their school vacation working in a Pioneer camp for a few days. The camp is in the woods very near the Moscow city line. Her husband, Misha, called Lera's parents and asked if she was home. The parents didn't know what he was talking about. The newlyweds had argued on Friday, and Lera left the camp around six in the evening and had not returned. Misha was sure that she had gone home to her parents. He wasn't in a hurry to call because he was angry.

The parents called all her friends. She wasn't anywhere. The police were searching the suburbs, and there's no news yet. Lera is a quiet homebody, and unexpected adventures are just not her style. What could have happened?

APRIL 6. The worst happened: She was found dead. The parents went to a parapsychologist and showed him her photograph. He said to look in water. There wasn't a river or lake near the camp, and the water is still half frozen anyway. The police went through the area once more and found her in a ravine in melted snow. She had been strangled, and scrapes on her side indicated that she had been dragged. There was no sign of rape. She had died six days ago, the day she left. Of course, they'll investigate and look for the killer. If he doesn't kill again, it will be almost impossible to find him. A friend suggested taking a closer look at the husband. He didn't like Misha's behavior; he had been very irritable from the start, always picking on Lera. Besides, how could he calmly stay at the camp for two and half days without knowing where his wife was?

It's hard even to write about Lera's parents. She was their only child, and a late one at that.

APRIL 9. It's amazing, but the death of a loved one actually gives you the strength to go on, freeing you from empty and meaningless emotions. Your existence takes on a more profound significance. Papa always loved Pushkin's lines "You understood life's goal: fortunate man, you live for life." My father always lived in expectation of life, forgetting to enjoy today. He knew that it was unnatural and destructive, but he couldn't change. Now Papa is gone, and gone with him are his expectations and often empty fears. I understood with morbid clarity—that's the end of life. The obituary in the newspaper, the empty desk at work, the empty room in our apartment, the things in his closet no one needs. He is with us, in the memory of his friends, and his name and unsullied reputation in science remain. But I remember his suffering, his dissatisfaction, his depression. I want so much to bring him back and say, "Look at your end. Why didn't you understand sooner that you have to value every day and live for life?"

The first shock, so piercing, and the almost unbearable pain are gone, and now I feel depression and sadness. Soon I learned that something had changed in me. I stopped paying attention to the squabbles and hassles at work, to the stupid words and empty threats from the idiot bosses. I understood that I wouldn't let "them" run my life anymore, stealing my happiness and peace of mind. Luckily, my inner freedom coincided with better times in the country. For the first time in decades people began to come out of their faint of fear and hopelessness. I am being given the chance my father never had. His world view was created by the times he lived in, which left almost no room for joy and optimism. How could I blame him for his lack of life wisdom?

CHAPTER NINE

On the Kaluga Wave

A taste of sadness in joy and sadness softened by humor or irony—
these are the spiritual states that I find most fruitful.

—FAZIL ISKANDER

APRIL 11. Yet another page of our Kaluga life has closed.
They called and told us that Uncle Misha, Papa's childhood
friend, had died. I could write a whole book about him and his
family—*The Wasted Life of Three Generations*. Uncle Misha's
father, Nikolai Mikhailovich, was a major financial figure before
the Revolution, the owner of several tea factories. When the
whole mess began, his wife and their oldest daughter managed
to escape to Harbin. The daughter later became a famous actress
and was known even in faraway America. Uncle Misha often
joked, "One day I'll get a call from the Foreign Legal Collegium,
and they'll tell me that my relatives left me a couple of million
dollars."

Nikolai Mikhailovich didn't manage to get out. He settled
in Kaluga and married the former governess of his children, a
Russified German. Their son Mikhail was born, half German,
half former capitalist and future Soviet prisoner camp inmate.
Nikolai Mikhailovich lived poorly but with dignity. He was
famous in the town for dressing with his former elegance and
wearing hats with great éclat. He earned money by playing a
violin in the city park. He died shortly before the war.

When the Germans entered Kaluga, Uncle Misha (as I called him) was working as a secretary in some office. He didn't leave his job during the brief occupation; he was his mother's sole support. After Kaluga was liberated, Uncle Misha was picked up right away, allegedly for collaboration with the Germans; his German antecedents did their work. He was sent to distant northern camps, where he spent ten years, the best years of his youth. After he got out, he settled in Ukhta, where many former inmates lived. By then his mother was long dead, and he had no place to go home. His lust for life prevailed, and he wanted a family. Uncle Misha married a rather strange woman who was ten years his senior. They had a son, whom they named in honor of his grandfather, Nikolai. Uncle Misha didn't love his wife much, so he gave all his attention to little Kolya, who grew up nervous and spoiled.

In the late fifties there was a wave of rehabilitation, and Uncle Misha decided to return to his hometown. As someone who had been illegally repressed, he was given a small one-bedroom apartment in Kaluga, which in those days was a gift of fate, if you could call that payment for his stolen youth a gift. He had a lot of trouble getting a job because the Soviet bosses still had suspicions of former political prisoners. After a few years Uncle Misha finished a technical school and got a job in a big factory. He worked in the supply department—that is, he used every means possible to get the parts the plant was legally entitled to. The most frequently used method was getting drunk with the officials, and the main currency was vodka. Without noticing it, Uncle Misha started drinking heavily. It must not have been an accident that Soviet reality finished what the camps had started, especially since his homelife wasn't very happy. In spite of all that, Uncle Misha retained his incredible optimism and vitality, and he was always joking and laughing. Talking about camp life, he recalled only the funny stories and sprinkled his tales with juicy camp slang. He was happy to have gotten out of there, and he didn't want to harp on the unpleasant times.

Uncle Misha had inherited his father's way with clothes. Even dead drunk on a garbage pile, he looked like a dandy. The drinking didn't spoil his taste for life and beauty. When he was sober, he read a lot and understood world politics, and it was always interesting to talk to him.

But fate kept at him. His son grew up and got mixed up with hooligans. One fine day they robbed a newspaper stand. They made off with small takings—some magazines, records, and pens—but they ended up in a colony for minors. It's a cruel system, and once you get in, it's hard to get out. When his term was over, Kolya spent a short time outside and then was arrested for some other small crime and ended up in a real prison. He spent fifteen years going back and forth. In the breaks between sentences, he managed to get married a few times and have children. I've heard strange stories about his prison life. He asked for an Esperanto dictionary and wanted to study the language. Then he began reading up on prerevolutionary Kaluga, and Uncle Misha raced around the used-book stores. Life brought Uncle Misha back into the past. And Kolya began drinking, too.

It was only in the last three years of his life that relative calm came to their house. Kolya came out of prison with the firm resolve not to return. I met Kolya last year. It was then that the idea of the wasted lives in the three generations came to me. Here was a tall, well-built young man who seemed sickly (he had lost a lung in a prison fight). Half his teeth had been knocked out and replaced with metal ones, and his arms were covered with tattoos. He looked the worse for wear. But when he started speaking, I forgot all that. He had a wonderful sense of current events, was a great admirer of Reagan and his hard policy toward the "evil empire." During *perestroika* Boris Yeltsin had become Kolya's idol. He even went to Moscow to hear him at rallies. But Kolya's heart belonged to prerevolutionary Russia. He knew the history of old Kaluga very well and could lead you down the small streets for hours, talking about the former life of the city and its residents. He preferred not to speak about his own life; that was an open wound. His prison past still had a hold on him. Whenever there is a robbery or other crime in the city, the police show up on his doorstep. "They won't leave me alone, as if I'm in their way. They'll put me away the first chance they get. I try not to go out too much," he said bitterly. I looked at his nervous face and thought that the Ukhta camps have a firm hold on their victims, even unto the next generation.

Now Kolya seems to be all right. He's stopped drinking, lives with his third wife and daughter, works in a factory, and breeds parrots.

Uncle Misha was found dead near his house early in the morning. He had been on his way home from the boiler plant where he worked as night watchman. It was amazing that he managed to live to the age of sixty plus, since he had had several strokes and was almost blind but still went on drinking heavily. He never did live to get that inheritance of millions from relatives abroad.

APRIL 13. I could tell a lot about the life of our courtyard and adjoining buildings in Kaluga. We had quite a few colorful characters. But I think I remember Uncle Zhenya, our courtyard singer, best. Uncle Zhenya was of medium height and rather thin, and his enormous, hawklike nose dominated his pale drinker's face. When he opened his mouth, he exposed his equine, rotting teeth. But as soon as he began singing, you forgot everything. Uncle Zhenya was a fair actor with charming provincial tricks. His repertoire was quite varied—from criminal songs to arias. Often, when the role demanded it, his voice broke with a threatened tear, and at the most dramatic moments real tears rolled down his sunken cheeks. He gave of his talent generously, performing a big concert every evening in the gazebo, and people from neighboring buildings came. Uncle Zhenya liked visiting us. He would sit in Grandfather's big armchair and sing with sweet, lachrymose feeling:

> The chrysanthemums in the garden have faded,
> But love still lives in my broken heart. . . .

He had problems with his own love life. His wife, Nurse Valya, was a shrew who sometimes even beat Uncle Zhenya. But you couldn't envy her life. They lived with their two sons in a small room, and they had almost no money. Valya watched Uncle Zhenya's morality closely, and one day she practically ruined his career as an actor. An operetta theater from a big Volga city was touring in Kaluga. The theater director happened to attend an amateur concert in which Uncle Zhenya performed, and he liked his fine tenor. Uncle Zhenya was offered a job at the theater for character parts. With his secret savings Uncle

Zhenya went to the store and bought a new suit. But Valya had forbidden him the theater, singing, and the corrupt life. Still, his attraction to the theater was stronger than his fear of his wife's threats. While everyone slept, Uncle Zhenya crept out the window in his new suit with a small suitcase in hand. His freedom didn't last. Valya caught him at the train station in the morning in a crowd of ladies from the operetta, only five minutes before the train left. The fugitive was returned to his family's bosom in shame.

Another threat happened later. After a short visit to Moscow, Uncle Zhenya kept talking about some woman named Frola. Valya grew nervous, but we knew that there was nothing to worry about. Here's the story. My parents took Uncle Zhenya to meet an elite group. Among the guests was the chic Flora, who later married a famous artist. The evening went very well, and Uncle Zhenya with his arias was the star. Flora enjoyed his songs and spent most of the evening dancing with the singer. Uncle Zhenya went crazy with happiness and was so nervous that he kept calling his lady Frola, getting the consonants reversed. At the end of the evening someone put our Caruso over his shoulder and left him out on the landing, where Papa found him fast asleep.

So Valya's life now passed under the sign of Frola. At the slightest provocation, Uncle Zhenya would threaten to go back to Moscow to Frola, who loved him and was a smart woman, a Ph.D. and not just a nurse. We didn't rat on Uncle Zhenya and watched developments; the whole neighborhood knew about Frola by now. At last Valya couldn't take any more and decided to go to Moscow to clear things up with Frola. Afraid of exposure, Uncle Zhenya shut up.

His life turned tragic. They moved to a big room in a communal flat. By then he was drinking heavily. He struck a neighbor in a drunken brawl, and the man almost died. What had the alcohol done to that sweet fellow who couldn't even shout at anyone? He spent many years in jail and returned a sick old man. And then his younger son, Igor, was put away. I don't even know if Uncle Zhenya is still alive.

APRIL 16. In the cultural sense Kaluga was far from the last city in prerevolutionary Russia. Famous scientists, artists, and writers were born and lived here. Today the city is best known for its connection with Konstantin Eduardovich Tsiolkovsky. His house, turned into a museum after his death, was not far from ours—left on Pushkinskaya and then down the steep street named after the scientist. When I was little, we often went to the museum. It didn't resemble a normal museum much, for it was a modest two-story building with all the furniture and fixtures in place, as if the owners had gone on a short trip. All the space and other technological exhibits didn't interest me. My attention was fixed on the cone-shaped metal tubes; you put the narrow part by your ear and the wide part toward the person speaking. Tsiolkovsky was hard of hearing, and that primitive apparatus helped him communicate with people. Legends abound about his life under Stalin. According to the official version, Tsiolkovsky hailed the Revolution gladly and started serving the welfare of young Soviet science wholeheartedly and selflessly. But I heard otherwise from Grandfather. Once he met a friend on the street who had just been to see Tsiolkovsky. He told Grandfather, "I keep trying to convince the old man to accept the Soviet regime, but he simply refuses."

My father saw Tsiolkovsky when he was a boy. He went with Grandfather to the man who did typing, and an old man with a long white beard was sitting on a chair in the corner. Grandfather whispered to Papa that it was the famous Tsiolkovsky. When the scientist died, Papa went with the other boys to Zagorodny Sad for the funeral, but it was so crowded that he didn't see a thing. By the way, the headstone on Tsiolkovksy's grave quotes wonderful things about Soviet rule that Konstantin Eduardovich allegedly spoke on his deathbed. The word in Kaluga is that he never said any such thing and that it was made up by his physician, who wanted to make the authorities happy.

The talented scientist Chizhevsky also lived in Kaluga. His life was tragic. He was endlessly harassed and persecuted, and his works were not published. Only recently has he been recognized, and his works are now in print and his research is studied. Once, a few years after the Revolution, Chizhevsky met my grandfather at the store, led him aside, looked around, and said in a whisper, "There's no hope; the Soviets have won conclusively."

Kaluga attracted people of the prerevolutionary generation in our day, too. Father's teacher, a native of St. Petersburg and a famous academician, enjoyed visiting our little house on Pushkinskaya Street. Using a cane, he walked up and down the streets, recalling his past. There was a period he did not like to discuss, the years in a Stalinist camp felling trees. I remember that he once said with a certain pride, "You know I have a great mastery of axes and saws." But strangely, he never criticized Stalin and did not allow political discussions in his house. As soon as the conversation turned in that direction, he interrupted and said, looking out the window, "Look at the pretty bird flying by." I don't know what it was, fear or caution.

He was quite an original character. He enjoyed tricking people or putting them in stupid situations. He wore an old leather coat in winter. Once, heading for Leningrad, he took an old backpack with him to the train station. As he approached the first-class car, he began burrowing in all his pockets for his ticket. The conductor looked him up and down and said, "Gramps, you're in the next car." "Gramps" walked away and came back with the ticket, handed it to the conductor with a bewildered air, and said that he couldn't understand what was going on. The conductor let the "bagman" academician into the car, and the old man enjoyed the scene he had created. He told us, by the way, that a backpack was perfect as a pillow.

But the story with the conductor was nothing compared with what he did once at an international scientific congress. Lunch was served during the break, and in typical Soviet style there were separate rooms for ordinary scientists and for professors and a special small room for academicians. Our academic entered the professors' room with feigned diffidence and sat at the table. A society lady, a professor's wife, who was one of the hostesses, hurried up to him and said, "Dearie, you're in the wrong place. You should be in that room," pointing to the room for ordinary scientists. He got up silently, went to that room, and came back to the woman. "They sent me back to you," he said. "They said academicians aren't supposed to be in there." The woman turned white with horror and burst into apologies. Throughout the lunch she came over every five minutes to ask if he needed anything. It was a terrific show.

APRIL 18. I think the time has come for me to describe an important meeting in my life. I kept putting it off, but the Kaluga reminiscences have given me confidence.

After my father died, Mama and I fulfilled a respectful and bitter duty: We met with Andrei Dmitrievich Sakharov. Papa had studied at Moscow University with him, when it was evacuated during the war deep into the rear. Later fate separated them. Papa became a famous specialist in his own field, and their scientific paths did not cross. He always followed Andrei Dmitrievich's scientific career closely and with pride and later suffered for him during his years of tragic exile in Gorky. Papa was tormented that he couldn't help or support him. Soviet power dealt ruthlessly with everyone who rose to Sakharov's defense. You had to be either very famous or absolutely fearless to put up with it. Papa was afraid—for all that he had achieved through honest and at times exhausting labor and for us. I'm not justifying his behavior. I just clearly understand how deep-seated that fear was because it is in my bones, too, to this day.

When Andrei Dmitrievich returned to Moscow, Mama asked my father if he wanted to see him, to recall their college days, and to express his support. Papa replied that it was too late now. It should have been done when Sakharov was alone and in trouble. He said it in a way that made it clear there could be no return to this conversation.

Still, we did return to it, but without Papa. We decided that we would tell Andrei Dmitrievich, "Yes, he really did want to see you, but he was afraid and in torment, but he was with you in his thoughts constantly."

Andrei Dmitrievich, with the sensitivity of a true member of the Russian intelligentsia, found time for us right away. I'm sure that it was not easy with the hectic pace of his new life. And so we went to the famous two-room apartment that was the cynosure of the world. Andrei Dmitrievich was dressed simply in a homey way—old jogging pants and a warm-up jacket. At first we spoke a bit about Papa and how his life had gone. Then we tried to tell him what we wanted to say gently without excessive emotion. Andrei Dmitrievich, of course, understood us, but we saw that Papa had been right: It was too late for him to come to Sakharov. He and his wife spoke bitterly about how alone they had been in those difficult days, when even their close friends turned away. I thought about the silent support of thousands of families like ours. But what good did that do them in those grim and courageous days? Andrei Dmitrievich said that the authorities had spread nasty and silly rumors about him and his wife, for instance, that he had been selling American jeans. "That's not so insulting; at least it's quality goods," I said attempting a little joke. He smiled.

Then we talked about what Papa had told us from his college years. They had lived on the verge of poverty in evacuation, with many of the students barefoot. At least they were in Central Asia, where it wasn't too cold. The auditoriums had signs, NO BAREFOOT STUDENTS MAY TAKE EXAMS. They borrowed shoes to go in for their orals. On graduation day Papa and Andrei Dmitrievich celebrated the event: They went to a mineral water vendor and got a glass each for a couple of kopecks. They added a few grams of wine to flavor it.

Papa was gone. He had worked up to the end. He couldn't believe that there were limits even for the strongest and hardest-working person. I asked Andrei Dmitrievich what he would prefer now: to continue his political activity or to pursue science and read books in the quiet of his apartment. He thought and replied, as if thinking aloud, that he probably preferred the latter. But it was clear that there would be no quiet study, that Andrei Dmitrievich had made his choice long ago and for the rest of his life. As we were leaving, Mama said that when the history of our age would be written, people would call it the Sakharov century.

A year later Andrei Dmitrievich tried to speak over the shouts of the "patriots" at the Congress. And in another six months after that he was gone.

APRIL 21. One of the components of our life in Kaluga was trips to the woods. As soon as it grew warm, we headed for the neighboring village of Annenki. Early in the morning Grandmother would pack food and worry about forgetting something. She always thought about details—what if someone's hot, or someone else is cold, or someone wants a candy and someone else wants something savory. All those possibilities made her pack several bags.

After breakfast my grandparents, my cousin, and I went off to Store No. 6 to wait for the suburban bus. The bus was almost always full, and we had to squeeze in. The woman conductor managed to maneuver through the crowd with amazing agility; a big leather bag with rolls of tickets of various colors hung from her shoulder. She had to tear off several tickets to get the right fare. The tickets cost mere kopecks.

After fifteen minutes of torture in the hot, bumpy bus we got off at the edge of the village. We headed for the wide road that led into the forest. I don't think any landscape is more Russian than that around Kaluga—mixed heavy forest, brush, high grass with lovely wild flowers. From time to time the forest cleared, and we entered a meadow. The meadows, especially on hot days, held the spicy, honey aroma of forest carnations. Bees buzzed, crickets chirped, my cousin and I tried to catch grasshoppers. I can shut my eyes and bring back all the sounds and smells. My skin can even feel the caressing warmth of the sun. I didn't feel nature as fully at any exotic beach on the Black Sea or the Mediterranean as I did in an ordinary Russian forest.

After walking for a couple of hours, we settled on the edge of a meadow in the shade. Grandmother took out blankets, laid out the food, and our feast began. It was never anything special—cucumbers, green onions, black bread, and meat patties, which Grandmother managed to keep warm by wrapping them in lots of paper. But everything tasted delicious outdoors, and our appetites were strong. We drank milk from little bottles. Each had his or her own. Grandmother used bottles that medicine had come in, corking them tightly and wrapping them in white paper, which somehow gave its taste to the milk. We had one ironclad rule: Never finish your milk; you might get thirsty on the way back.

After the meal we stretched out luxuriously on the blankets. Grandfather often told us stories from his life. He had an astonishing memory; for instance, he could tell you what had happened that day twenty years ago. He could recite entire Chekhov stories by heart and chapters from Jules Verne's books. In addition, he knew more than five foreign languages. He had learned German and French at school and English, Italian, and Spanish on his own. He also knew Esperanto, but he didn't talk too much about that, since for decades Esperanto speakers were persecuted in the Soviet Union and put into camps as potential spies. It was amazing that Grandfather hadn't been arrested under Stalin since he fitted all the requirements: noble birth, good education, member of the intelligentsia. Apparently he was saved by living a poor and unnoticed life, so that he had no envious enemies. Perhaps God preserved him, for Grandfather was profoundly devout. His inner spiritual wealth helped him retain his vivacity even at the grimmest and most tragic times. I think his love of nature helped too. He was a different man in the forest, imbued with special energy.

After lying in the grass, we headed on, with lighter packs. Grandfather was a tireless traveler, despite his bad leg. When I was very little, thieves got into the room on Pushkinskaya Street. Trying to catch them, Grandfather jumped out the window and broke his leg. Ever since then it was always swollen and often hurt, so that he had to use a cane. It was from Grandfather that I learned to feel and understand nature. He didn't teach us anything in particular. He simply walked, limping down the paths and pointed to trees, flowers, berries, anthills with his cane and told us the names of things and about the animals living in the woods. He loved butterflies—with a Nabokovian passion. On the way back we picked heaps of wild flowers so that the apartment was filled with forest scents in the evening. Often the flowers lasted until our next expedition.

Sometimes we took longer trips. The best place was the Polotnyayny factory, the former Goncharov estate. What remained of the good old days was the huge park. At one time the regional party boss tried to have the age-old trees chopped down, but fortunately there were more trees than workers.

The house burned down, and only ruins remained of the once-beautiful building. It's still not clear what happened. The official version is that the Germans burned down the house during the war. But the locals said that it was Russians who did it before the war. There had been a museum in the estate, and village drunks got into the room filled with various oddities and monsters kept in alcohol. They broke the jars and drank the alcohol. They might have burned down the house, too, to cover their tracks.

It was sad to see how Russians were destroying their own culture. Pushkin had come here. The estate belonged to his wife's relatives, and he had walked in the old park, sat in the gazebo, and regarded the bend in the river and the fields and forests stretching to the horizon. It was here that he wrote:

The east is covered in rosy dawn,
And in the distance beyond the river, a light went out.

We wanted to be transported to the nineteenth century, to see the old house, and to walk through its charming grounds. Now I would love to return for a bit to my Kaluga childhood, but it is as inaccessible as the nineteenth century.

APRIL 24. When I think about Kaluga, I can't leave out the story of my great-aunt, Grandfather's stepsister. We became real friends when she realized that I liked the decadent poets. This made me worthy of her attention. No, she wasn't a snob. It's just that her romantic illusions were stronger than reality to the

last day of her life. It was probably these illusions that complicated her life, but she never complained of her choice. She was
married rather early to a young man with a good future. "He
loved me so much," she told me, "that he often took off my
shoes and kissed my toes. And my feet, by the way, weren't all
that clean," she added with a chuckle. She left her husband after
several years, to run off with a handsome actor. He couldn't
give her anything besides love, and that she had to share with
other women. But Auntie didn't complain about her fate. She
loved her new husband and was prepared to forgive him everything. They spent most of their life in a tiny room in a communal
flat. When we visited them, there weren't enough chairs for
everyone. But Auntie continued stubbornly to live in her own
world. She read decadents, listened to love songs, and bred cats.
In the meantime, her first husband had made his way in the
world. His new family lived in a big three-bedroom apartment
and shopped in stores for the privileged. Auntie always fried up
some cheap fish on a gas ring when we came to call.

Auntie's daughter got married, and one more person moved
into the tiny room. The newlyweds slept on a folding cot. The
son-in-law was a simple worker, kind and receptive. Auntie
quickly converted him. He started reading poetry and came to
like the old love songs. It was funny to see the big, broad fellow
reading the exquisite and mannered poems of Gumilev.

Today, I see, your gaze is particularly sad,
And your arms, embracing your knees, are particularly thin.
Listen, far, far away along Lake Chad
Wanders an exquisite giraffe.
It is given graceful slender and languor,

And a magical pattern adorns its skin,
With which only the moon dares to compare,
Shattering and swaying on the moisture of broad lakes. . . .

Auntie got two presents late in life: a small one-bedroom apartment and *The Master and Margarita*, published in *Moskva* journal at long last. I don't know which was more important to her. She held on to Bulgakov's novel to the very end. The night before she died, Auntie's daughter read to her from her beloved book until morning.

A few years ago I was in Tallinn at the grave of the poet Igor Severiyanin. I read the lines quoted on his headstone and thought of Auntie:

How beautiful and fresh will be the roses
My country will toss into my coffin.

APRIL 25. One fine morning the front door opened, right into the entry room where my cousin and I slept in warm weather, and a young foreign-looking man stood on the doorstep. This was in the sixties, when America was on another planet as far as we were concerned. Kostya, the son of our friends, was wearing American jeans, a jersey with bright lettering, and big crocodile-leather shoes. He had a name brand bag filled with records and foreign clothes slung over his shoulder. The twenty-year-old had come from Moscow to visit his relatives and have some fun. We were handy—a fun group. At breakfast he told us that he was in his American period. He would buy American clothes and records and stuff, and sometimes to get the complete feeling, he would walk in front of the American Embassy, paying no mind to the vigilant police outside. With charming sincerity, Kostya told us that he was tired of his Jewish period and liked his new role better. During the Jewish period he told everyone that he and his mother were poor Jews who had been abandoned by his father and were eking out a miserable existence. He was no more Jew than American, but the trusting provincials believed him and helped out. Some gave clothes, some a few jars of home preserves, and some gave money. "Now, in my American period, the income is better and life is more fun," Kostya confided. Of course, we realized that the enterprising youth was a simple black marketeer.

After breakfast he had to get out and around; he was looking for fun. Kostya took out some American T-shirts for us from his bag and said that we'd go walk around town pretending to be foreigners. This was in Kaluga, where no foreigners were allowed.

To start with, we pretended we were Poles. We stopped at a mineral water stand, and Kostya asked with a Polish accent how to get to Red Street. We said nothing and even had a second free glass of water; the woman wanted to treat the "furreners." We reached Red Street, where Kostya's aunt lived. He turned into a poor relative again and got a big three-liter jar of strawberry jam. Once he saw that he wouldn't get anything else out of her, he claimed he had to catch a train. Then the most interesting part began. It was time for us to be Americans. We decided to go to the city park, where there were always lots of people and we would have an audience. A flower show was being held in the former church in the middle of the park. His prior victories gave him no peace, and Kostya decided to be Jewish, this time from Israel, and told us to speak English. My cousin could do all right, but I hadn't gotten much beyond "beautiful" and "wonderful" after several years of English at school. We walked around the room and expressed our delight with our limited vocabulary. Kostya went up to the elderly man in charge of the exhibit and in broken Russian with a Jewish accent told him that he was a tourist from Israel and that we were American students crazy about lovely Kaluga and that we wanted to leave a note in the visitors' book. Kostya spoke loudly so that everyone could hear. In a few minutes a small crowd had gathered, and the women looked at our clothes with interest. Kostya, to our amazement, wrote something in Hebrew, and my cousin put together a few sentences in English.

"Good-bye, good-bye," we cried as we showered them with air kisses. After we had left the church, Kostya sighed and said that he had almost been caught. He thought that the man in charge actually was Jewish and would expose him to his great shame. He had a lot of trouble pretending to write in Hebrew. Kostya kept thinking, *He's going to find out and show me up.* I still don't understand how the trusting Kalugans could have fallen for Kostya's cheap trick.

It would have all been fun and cute if it hadn't turned to something uglier when Kostya grew older. He sold out and became a scoundrel. He chose another role for himself later. He took a job in a factory and became "an honest Soviet citizen and a militant patriot." When Solzhenitsyn was thrown out of the Soviet Union, Kostya went on TV in the name of "simple laborers" and applauded that "just act" and condemned the "traitor." I wonder what Kostya's up to now, and what camp he joined in the days of *perestroika*.

APRIL 27. My Kaluga childhood must have seemed too happy and cloudless because my family tried not to tell us the bad things, first of all, to protect our childlike innocence, and secondly, because they were afraid to. No one could be certain that the bad times wouldn't return.

Grandmother got letters occasionally from Siberia and wept when she read them. The letters were from her brother, who had been sent to Siberia when the NEP (New Economic Policy, a return to capitalism, instituted by Lenin in 1921) was attacked. He was exiled for nothing: for working and showing initiative. In exile he married out of despair, unhappily, and had children and lived in dire straits. I saw him once not long before his death. I remember a tall, thin man with a sad face, who said only a few words at the dinner table. The fate of Grandmother's brother was always a painful spot for the family, but there wasn't much they could do for him. He was so mired in his lost life.

No one in our family died in the Stalinist camps and prisons, but that tragedy did befall someone close to us, the wife of Father's brother. When she was twelve, her father was arrested. He was the director of a large Soviet institution, a nobleman who had accepted the Revolution and served it loyally. It destroyed him. In the infamous year of 1937, the height of the

Great Terror, he was shot, but his family thought he was alive in the camps and waited for his return for many years. In 1940 my aunt wrote a poem—she was only fifteen.

It is evening, it is so quiet here, I am alone with an open
    book.
I recall at midnight everything that seemed to be
    forgotten.
And unconsciously poetry on my lips, that strange,
    sorrowful Esenin.
One lamp is lit, and grim shadows stir in the corners.
In the sky, clear outlines of rooftops, the jangle of trolleys
    dies out in the distance,
And once again un-Moscow–like silence, with only a sad
    violin playing.
Somewhere beyond the mountains my forgotten father
    lives.
The distant image comes to my eyes, the violin sings
    sadly and softly.
Those agitating and tender sounds give rise in my dreams
To him strong, bold, sitting casually with a cigarette in
    his handsome hands.
My father, beloved tenderly and bitterly, with his piercing
    eyes.
The familiar image blurs, do you ever think of us at all?
In the sky, clear outlines of rooftops, the jangle of trolleys
    dies out in the distance,
And once again the un-Moscow–like silence, the violin
    grieving and weeping.

But he couldn't miss them since he had been dead for several years by then. After the Twentieth Congress of the party (when Khrushchev revealed the crimes of the Stalin regime) he was posthumously rehabilitated and reinstated in the party. It's amazing what this so-called triumph of justice did for the family. My aunt and her mother became even more fervent Communists, and the death of their father and husband became a mere historical error. My aunt was also a militant atheist, but in the last years she saw more, either because she became wiser with age or because the truth that came pouring out from all sides at us had its effect. Now she is a believer but doesn't attend church because she is ailing and housebound. She still writes poetry; one poem is dedicated to her parents.

Their trespasses will be forgiven, they will reap what they
    sowed,
For their cares and worries and hearts they gave to us.
For their suffering in this life, for their dreams in vain,
For their love of their homeland, forgive them, Lord, forgive.
And I pray meekly that you forgive me, too, for everything,
And for my wrongdoing, dear God, I repent so bitterly.

Many believe that the rebirth of our country will come from the repentance of every individual.

APRIL 30. In his *Essays* Montaigne quoted in Latin, "So man must always wait for his very last day, and no one can be called happy before his death and funeral service." In other words, even at the very end of your life things may happen that could turn you from a happy person to the most miserable and vice versa.

I've often wondered if my grandparents could be called happy. Probably. All their adult, conscious life they lived in difficult and sometimes tragic times. Yet they remained alive and died natural deaths at an old age in their beds. They did not outlive their sons. Their sons did not die at war or in the camps. They did not pay for the right to survive the horrible Stalin years with treachery or denunciations, like the many people who were forced to slander others when it was a question of life and death. The Lord gave them strong faith in atheistic times. Their faith must have helped them maintain their sense of dignity and love of life in their modest and often impoverished and unnoticed existence. God gave my grandfather many talents and at the same time protected him from the desire to show off those talents, thereby saving him. That is the tragic paradox of twentieth-century Russia.

CHAPTER TEN 🍂

Every Psycho
Has a Program

Whatever you like will drive you crazy.
—RUSSIAN FOLK SAYING

MAY 2. A friend of ours has an amusing theory: Everything that goes beyond elementary needs is a deviation from the norm. For instance, a woman's desire to cook delicious food is normal, but the desire to dress well and be attractive is unnatural. He himself is a mass of extremes—total asceticism in life except for gastronomic refinement, economizing on every ruble but buying antique rarities for enormous sums. In his daily life he is very eccentric. I once went to his place and found the following scene: He was walking around in shorts (it was winter) in a chilly room. A canary was perched on a lamp, with newspapers spread beneath it since the bird's behavior was not very civilized. The room, which he had just acquired by trading with his brother, was remarkably furnished: a narrow camp bed, a simple wooden table and chairs from the fifties, and lots of camping equipment hanging on the walls. The bookshelves, which took up half the room, were filled with rare editions. There was also a painting by a famous eighteenth-century artist. With no curtains the window showed the black night, and the small pane was open to let in a stream of icy air. He walked around energetically from time to time, to keep from freezing. Fortunately the teakettle whistled, and I was saved from a cold grave. The kitchen was warm, and he put lots of good food on the table. Rene Georgievich (the name alone is priceless) ate silently and with great concentration, embodying one of his theories: Cooking is a special art worthy of great respect; therefore, consuming food should be done wholeheartedly and undistractedly. From time to time we did exchange a few remarks about the food's quality.

Back in his room (I meekly asked him to close the window) we talked about everything under the sun. The man has an incredible quality: He emancipates your brain. We talked about the most varied things, and he always found his own twist on them. He has a phenomenal memory, especially about books. In the good old days he would have made a marvelous used-book store owner and would have been famous all over Moscow. Nothing is right in our society. It doesn't value original and unusual people. He has good reason not to go into the used-book business now. It's a slippery business, and you can get into trouble fast. By the way, Rene Georgievich is a professor. He teaches at an institute, but I think he would give up everything for his books. He dresses very bizarrely, as if he wanted to shock, but it's just that he's truly more comfortable that way. He's not so bad now, but he wore the same coat for twenty years and in summer went around in funny sweatpants and carrying a woman's shopping bag. Of course, none of that is important, and the charm of his mind and personality makes you forget his eccentricities. My knowledge of literature and painting comes

from him. He spent so much time with me in bookstores, back
when you could still find things to buy; half my large library was
collected thanks to his efforts! You can call him at any moment
and learn about the most interesting exhibits and concerts in
Moscow. He also plays the piano well. So according to his own
theory, he's abnormal, a real schizophrenic.

MAY 5. By the way, I heard that expression about the psycho
from another friend who clearly considers himself part of that
merry band. He obviously means a pleasant eccentric, an original, not like everyone else. But I think he's overestimating himself. He lives too well in our society. Psychos and eccentrics
don't flourish here. They lack the calculation and flexibility to
blend into the Soviet system. Often their eccentricity is a way
of getting away from the reality of our life into their own world.

Take Oleg Vladimirovich, for instance. He really belongs
in Geneva or New York. It's not clear why every time someone
else gets to go instead of him. He graduated from the diplomatic
academy and is fluent in a foreign language, but he must not
have the connections. He is, however, famous for his collection
of *National Geographic*. He has several decades' worth at home.
So he travels in his armchair, as that magazine recommends.
Oleg Vladimirovich is an Anglophile. He even resembles an
Englishman—tall, thin, and conservatively dressed. He always
has oatmeal, made with water, and a steak for breakfast. He
insists that the meat be cut against the grain. Of course, it's a
moot point since we don't have meat nowadays.

He has a mysterious weakness: He's a confirmed bachelor. So is Rene Georgievich. It's strange. In Moscow there are many excellent potential brides and grooms, but you can never get them together. Recently we tried to marry off Oleg Vladimirovich, and here's what happened. A friend of mine saw him at my place and started sharpening her skis, as we say. She's a practical girl and knew that he could be made into a good husband. At first everything went well. We invited them over together another time and disappeared into the kitchen at the right moment. When we returned, they were holding hands (he hadn't even noticed how his hands had ended up in those tender handcuffs). Then she got sick in a very timely manner, and he visited her and brought flowers and fruit. Marina was already planning her wedding dress. She even wondered how a man like him was still running around free. And suddenly it became clear: His mother, with whom he lived, was against all women. When little Oleg disobeyed, she beat up her forty-year-old baby. When Marina, talking to Oleg Vladimirovich on the phone, heard him fending off his jealous mother, her dreams vanished. We saw that he had been in his mother's power too long to get rid of her now. It's a shame, for he's a fine, intelligent, and talented man.

Many of my friends wonder why I'm not in the marriage market. My own program is enough for me. Two programs would be much too much.

MAY 10. Here's a truly tragicomic matrimonial story, a modern Soviet plot for Gogol. Tatyana Leonidovna has a lot of trouble with suitors. She's a strange one, hoping to find a good husband in our day. She doesn't want much, a kind, intelligent man, so that she's not so lonely. Tatyana Leonidovna, by the way, is an attractive blonde of fifty and a university professor. But all her suitors are more impressed by her wealth than her distinctions. She has a beautiful old apartment in the center of Moscow with antique furniture and a big dacha outside town. There are no heirs because her first marriage was childless. The men quickly figure out what's what. Once she had to call a friend to help get rid of one such suitor. This time she is in real trouble. She hadn't called us in several months, and suddenly we heard the news: She's married. He is also a professor of mathematics. At first things were going well, with just one exception: He refused to sleep with her. He said that he had to get used to it. But this was an important aspect for Tatyana. She is a woman in her prime. In short, her eyes gradually opened. The new husband, named Leopold, is busy at the dacha and showing an unhealthy interest in her antiques, asking about their provenance and price. His grown sons are doing the same. Tatyana is nervous, losing sleep, and is carefully tasting her food, afraid of being poisoned. We had a talk and decided that it was time to get rid of him. Her apartment has a separate dark entrance, and the first-floor windows open onto an empty courtyard. He could hire thugs to bump her off.

I've decided one must be careful with one's boyfriends. I don't have any particular treasures, but I do have a good library. It doesn't take much anymore.

MAY 13. Tatyana's so-called husband has revealed himself completely. There's no doubt that he's a fortune hunter. A day after our last conversation she asked him to leave the house, and he did reluctantly. Two days later he called, and she said she was going on a business trip. Actually she wasn't going anywhere and had in fact invited a woman friend to stay with her. Just a few hours later there was a warning ring of the doorbell. The two women were prepared. Tatyana hid behind the door while her friend answered. Seeing the friend, Leopold started shouting at her and accusing her of theft. He tried to push his way into the apartment. When that failed, he went away, threatening to call the police. In the meantime, Tatyana called the police herself. Leopold returned in ten minutes with his police and asked them to take away the alleged criminal who was in the apartment while the lady of the house was away. At the right moment Tatyana appeared triumphantly, asked what the noise was all about, and introduced her friend to the guardians of law and order. The police checked the owner's passport, saw that she was registered to live there, and relaxed. Leopold was stunned, but his ignominy was just beginning. The police Tatyana had called arrived. Now his passport was checked, and he wasn't registered to live there. Fortunately she hadn't registered him. Now he was the domestic hooligan. The friend told the police how he had shouted and threatened and tried to get into the apartment. Leopold left in shame.

Today Tatyana Leonidovna went to a lawyer who told her to file for divorce immediately. He told her that Leopold still had a chance of wresting away some of her property even though the marriage was not consummated. Who would care whether he slept with her or not at that age? He'd just say he was impotent. Maybe he was. Tatyana Leonidovna should have found out before she got married, but he had played at being an old-fashioned gentleman, which she liked. She's paying for her dreamy naïveté and acting like a nineteenth-century maiden.

MAY 20. I keep complaining about how bad life is in Moscow, but I should remember the people who live in small provincial towns. I'd go crazy there. People live there and find joy, and some live with more dignity than those in the capital. One of the best ways is to give up on reality and live in your own world, like our dear friend Vladislav Aleksandrovich. Outside his window is a dreary little town with muddy streets, empty stores, and drunkards all around, but he travels between ancient Rome and the Middle Ages and conquers the meaninglessness and hopelessness of his surroundings. His favorite spot is a used-book store. Over many years of hunting for books he has created a unique library. And he speaks differently somehow—simply and with refinement, as if he had been transported from the educated nineteenth century. His every visit to our place is a banquet for the soul and mind. He is a very tactful and even shy man, and he not only doesn't show off his knowledge, but practically apologizes for it. It is not his goal so much as a way of life. The dynasty of French kings is more real to him than the members of the Soviet government. For every contemporary event he has a historical analogy, and for him our society is always associated with the fall of the Roman Empire. I wonder if the analogies help when he is running from store to store in search of chicken, meat, and other foodstuffs. On every trip to

Moscow he has an assignment: to get several weeks' food for his wife and children. When he finishes his scholarly business, he bustles through the stores and then goes to the railroad station to leave his purchases at the baggage hold. By the time he's ready to leave he has a good selection that he loads onto the train. He often comes to our apartment with his latest find, which he keeps in the refrigerator while we have our intellectual talks. He jokes about these foraging problems as if they didn't affect him.

Actually Vladislav Aleksandrovich is a pessimist who long ago gave up any hope of changing real life. He is a talented scholar with a famous name, but his honesty and even morbid decency kept him from making a career, since scholarship often goes hand in hand with selling out. So he sits in his godforsaken town, making scholarly discoveries, reading books, and waiting for the Roman Empire to fall, since he knows for sure how it will happen.

MAY 24. I'm sure he's an artist of genius, but as Vladimir Vysotsky's song goes, "Let them try it, I'll wait." Last night's adventure was more than enough for me. Ivar came to see me around six, and with typically Baltic politeness he gave me lovely roses, kissed my hand, and said pretty compliments. Then he told me about his fourth wife, whom he loves very much. He falls in love from time to time and gets married. Ivar feels it is indecent to cheat on women just as it is indecent to sleep with them outside marriage. So in his thirty-five years he has had three divorces and three children. Ivar likes to get all his children together and take them to the park. This doesn't happen too often because he works like a fanatic. I must say that he paints wonderful things. I am convinced that he will be famous some day.

So we had dinner, drank some wine, and, as usual, talked about many things. Friends who live in the building next door called and invited us over. Ivar, who is not very sociable, agreed and told me that he was in the mood to drink. He has the strange ability to program himself: "Today I work until I pass out; tomorrow I party without limits." At first things went well. We drank moderately and for fun, talking and enjoying ourselves, but suddenly Ivar changed. He got completely drunk in a second. We decided to take him outside and put him in a taxi to drive him home, but we couldn't. He resisted and pushed my friend, who was trying to hold him up and keep him from falling in the snow. We realized that we couldn't get him into a taxi, so we took him to my place. I saw how hard male friendships are; you can't leave a drunken pal in the snow. The neighbor turned out to be a weakling. He got us to the elevator and ran off. It's a good thing that Ivar is slight. I couldn't have managed with a big man. He collapsed on the couch and begged me to close the doors. "They'll come for me; lock up tight." But the doors were closed.

I suggested he go to sleep, but he told me in slurred words that he had to brush his teeth. I could understand that. I never went to bed without brushing my teeth, even in former merry days when I could have been drunk. Before he reached the sink, Ivar fell into the tub. I was furious, but at the same time it was funny. I got him out and set him up by the sink. I handed him a toothbrush. He brushed long and methodically while I held him up. Then we had a problem. He needed to use the toilet. He suggested that I hold him up from behind while he did what he needed. That was too much. I stood him up by the toilet, leaned him against the wall, and told him what to do. I went out and waited for the sound of a falling body. No problem. A few minutes later he was dead to the world in my bed. I took the folding bed and thought this was what it was like with an alcoholic husband, dealing with this every night. There are so many miserable women like that in our country! I felt lucky. Ivar would leave in the morning, and I would joke with my friends about this. Actually he thought it was funny, too, and in the morning he wanted all the details—what he had done, what he had said. I told him about the windows and doors and asked him what the problem was. I could see that it was serious and sad. He is terrified of ending up in jail because he won't be able to paint. "And I'll die if I can't paint," he confessed.

"But why would they want to put you in jail?" I asked.

He said that in our country the authorities can put you away for no reason; they could just do it. That's why he's so afraid of open doors, especially when he's been drinking. He thinks that they are coming up the stairs after him and getting closer to the door. And he drinks sometimes to get rid of his tension and fears. When he told me this, I remembered one of his paintings: twilight, a solitary man standing knee-deep in the snow in a field and looking at a grim, half-deserted village in the distance. The picture is imbued with depression, loneliness, and despair. You can't paint a picture like that without feeling it all in the depths of your soul.

MAY 26. I have these extravagant impulses sometimes. I see a painting or read a poem and I have the need to travel. Once I went to Tallinn after contemplating Breughel. I wanted to experience medieval Europe. And just the other day I was reading Mandelstam . . . :

> I have returned to my city, familiar as tears,
> As my sinews, as childhood's swollen glands.
> Petersburg, I do not want to die yet,
> I have your telephone numbers.

. . . and realized that I couldn't resist. I had to go to Petersburg-Leningrad. Mama decided to go with me. After all, it's her hometown. It's a good thing we have a friend at the ticket counter. We can pick up our tickets tomorrow. I don't know what we'd do without her. There are no tickets available nowadays.

Tatyana Leonidovna called with a new mystery episode. Leopold called and asked for the keys to the dacha (which she had wisely taken away from him). He said he had to pick up his clothes. She said she was busy and couldn't meet him. She went off to the dacha, gathered up his things, and took a taxi to his place with a friend. She waited downstairs, and her girl friend went up to his floor, rang his doorbell, and offered Leopold a bag with his stuff. He shouted that he didn't want to deal with her and slammed the door. Then she knocked at the neighbor's door and asked him to give the bag to Leopold, who must have been listening at his door, because he leaped out and yelled at the neighbor not to take the things. But the friend was running down the stairs by then. Now they don't know what happened to the bag.

Leopold called Tatyana as if nothing had happened and tried to persuade her not to get a divorce. He said that she was too impulsive and temperamental, while he was rational and controlled, just the kind of man she needed. Now he's going around telling all his friends how much he adores her and doesn't want to lose her. But Tatyana Leonidovna knows his tricks, and she took the final papers to the court. The denouement approaches.

JUNE 2. So we're back from Leningrad. I returned with a strange feeling: Something is rotten in that kingdom. I even said to Mama, "It's like coming back from a madhouse to a normal one." I recently heard that Leningraders think the same about us.

They say that Leningrad is turning into a ghost town. I think that's an amazingly accurate description. The old Petersburg streets are there, the magnificent buildings, the embankments—you can touch them, they're here, but they're not, not really. The unique spirit of Petersburg is gone, leaving only the shell, which is beginning to fall apart, like a corpse. Walking through the city, you seem to be at a gigantic surrealistic funeral. I may be exaggerating, but I want to convey the acuteness of my sensations. Small provincial towns in Russia die with a gentle sadness, but Petersburg is losing its majesty heavily and grimly. I think that the people there are strange, too. They seem to be trying to escape from reality.

The first thing we did was visit Mama's childhood friend. She has a big apartment in the center of town, with long hallways, tall ceilings, and windows facing a dark well of a courtyard. Irina Nikolayevna and her son live in that apartment as if it were a fortress. I think they try not to go out more than necessary. The son is a talented physicist, a professor, who works mostly at home and goes to his institute only a few times a week. So they wander around the apartment like ghosts, going to sleep at dawn and getting up at noon. They spend hours drinking tea in the kitchen. They look out at the courtyard with great curiosity: who went by, with whom, when. They need some impressions from the world around them. The son spends most of his time in his study reading. He has a marvelous library. Artyom isn't so old, but he has no plans to marry. He's stopped all communications with women—too many problems. "You have to get dressed up, leave the house; it's cold outside. And then you have to figure out where to go, how to amuse the lady. I don't even answer the phone anymore. I'm tired of fighting off pushy women," Artyom explained.

I can understand the ladies. He's good-looking, well educated, a good conversationalist, and a professor to boot—the perfect bridegroom. But he's a hopeless case; he won't marry. And he's turned to religion of late. He goes to church twice a day, reads religious philosophy, and observes all the fasts and Lenten days.

We spent about two hours at their place until I felt the need to go outside, to see light and hear the city noises. Mama and I walked in the street and wondered why their lives had taken such a strange turn. We decided that Irina Nikolayevna was much to blame. She has an abnormal, morbid love for her son. She wants to possess him, not share him, and she's the one who told him that he didn't need women, that they bring nothing but trouble. She is afraid that if Artyom married, he would pay less attention to her. Well, I'm not going to judge them, but it's sad to see a young, brilliant man letting life pass him by. Perhaps, though, he's happy in his own world. At least Soviet reality barely touches him.

The next day I went to see some bohemian friends of my artist friends in Moscow. I got there around one o'clock, and they were just getting up. Volodya was combing his long hair in front of the mirror; then he made a ponytail and put a dangling earring in one ear. His girl friend, Tanya, came out of the bathroom to say hello. There were sketches scattered all over the place. You couldn't even see the floor. There were also pages of an avant-garde novel that Volodya has been writing for several years. Rare books, primarily on philosophy, stood on the shelves.

We went into the kitchen to have breakfast. I had bought fresh rolls on the way, and Volodya and Tanya were thrilled; they had nothing but oatmeal and herb tea in the house. Volodya made the hot cereal with great expertise. It was obviously their main sustenance. The kitchen was a mess; I tried not to look around. A friend of Volodya's, who works at Leningrad University, dropped by. Volodya plumped the pot of oatmeal on the dirty oilcloth, put out my rolls, and the party began. I must say that the herbal tea was delicious, but the oatmeal was not very appetizing. There was a grayish film on top which worried the friend. Volodya kept pushing it aside with a spoon and insisting that it was perfectly edible. The oatmeal was all anyone talked about for the first ten minutes. Then the show started. The boys told me about their merry lives and grandiose plans. Petersburg was in a renaissance, they maintained. It was a time of complete freedom. Everything was bubbling and boiling. It was time for the young to take power and establish complete intellectual and creative freedom.

"For starters we will separate Vasilyevsky Island and turn it into something like the Crimea. Of course, there will be no Soviet power there, and we'll keep away from politics. We'll get the best people. We'll write books, paint, amuse ourselves a bit, and live the way we want," Volodya told me, greedily eating my rolls. Tanya was very quiet. I think she was still half asleep. Soon the conversational euphoria got to me. The boys were so excited about their plans. I began offering my ideas for the new life and asked them to reserve a place for me on the island.

"Of course," Volodya assured me. "You're part of our crowd, even if you are from Moscow." We decided to celebrate our new alliance. Volodya ran down to the café on the first floor and returned with a portion of whipped cream. The waitresses know him well and give him credit. But he's had too much debt there lately, and he could get only one portion. We divided it up fairly and ate it. Two hours passed without my noticing. I didn't want to go back to real life. As I stood in the doorway, a few more people showed up, and I was introduced as a Moscow candidate for the free Vasilyevsky Island. I went outside, but for some reason I didn't feel the wind of freedom blowing. I thought about how lucky these sweet and lazy young people were because even in Brezhnev's day, when there were so many informers around, talk like theirs could have landed them in prison. Now you can say whatever you want. We've been talking and talking for several years, yet so little has changed.

I felt very sad about three days into my visit. Every corner of Leningrad used to be magical for me. The names alone enchanted me: Liteyny, Fontanka, Taurida Gardens, Nevsky. What happened? Had I changed, gotten old? I walked around the city, looking at the crumbling buildings no one was restoring, and recalled the wonderful days I had spent in this city. I never did figure it out—why Leningrad had become alien for me, why the people seemed strange. For the first time in my life I left Leningrad without regrets. On the contrary, I was fleeing without a backward look.

JUNE 6. Everything is fun in Moscow, gallows humor, of course. Lots of people feel terrible, and they're trying to cheer themselves up. We have a gloomy friend whose life is not the happiest. He's almost completely without work, is divorced, and doesn't like the Soviet system. Vsevolod is a wise and subtle man, but extremely unenterprising. Maybe life made him that way because he saw there was no point in trying. He calls sometimes and complains about his life, making me incredibly depressed, and then suddenly his voice gets a lift in it, and he reels off a series of slightly improper jingles:

A star fell from heaven right into my lover's pants.
It could blow everything up in there, as long as there's no war.

Vsevolod enjoys this a lot and forgets his troubles.

The old lady didn't suffer long in the high voltage wires.
Her charred body was found in the bushes.

Grandpa found a grenade in the bushes.
He went to the party committee with it.
He lobbed it into the window.
Grandpa is old, he doesn't care.

He likes jokes about Soviet life, involving Pioneers (like Boy
Scouts) and October kids (Cub Scouts).

Stars, ribbons, shoes in a row.
The trolley ran over an October kids' squad.

Children played Gestapo in the cellar,
And tortured Potapov the plumber to
death.

He has an inexhaustible supply, and he tells me new ones
every time I see him.

A widow strolled in the leafy park with a Pioneer.
The widow felt sorry for the Pioneer and gave in to him.

This is followed by another quatrain, and at the end there comes
an explanation of why she slept with the lad:

Because in our country today everyone is young
In our glorious Soviet land.

I have the feeling that he writes them with his pals at work. Vsevolod is a translator of a rare language that is not popular in Moscow now. The Communist movement in that country has collapsed, and the works of the classics of Marxism-Leninism, which he used to translate, are not in demand. There are lots of people like Vsevolod at his job because the net of our propaganda is very wide, and more countries keep falling out. In expectation of better times the translators are kept on and paid salaries. So they wander from room to room and amuse themselves as best they can since they have to put in the time. I think it's wonderful that they are keeping the oral folk arts alive.

JUNE 10. My neighbor seems to be created especially for the pages of this diary. The famous accountant Berlaga in the novel *The Twelve Chairs* by Ilf and Petrov hid out from Soviet authorities in a mental institution. Our neighbor Petya hasn't reached that point yet, but he does have a certificate from the psychiatric and neurological clinic. As soon as he has a problem, he shows his boss the paper: "I'm not completely healthy, so leave me alone." That way Petya avoided the army and other unpleasant things. He actually is a danger to our society; he thinks too much and understands too deeply. He once told me jokingly, "I think they should pay me money to stay home and not bother anyone. I'd be much more useful that way." To tell the truth, Petya is very lazy and likes to stay home and read. He and his wife have lived in their apartment for five years, and they still haven't set up the furniture or hung curtains. That's not important; it's even exotic. I like going to their place, for we can certainly talk there about everything. Petya, by the way, is a parapsychologist; he predicts the future and has healing powers. He predicts many things accurately. It's always a pleasure spending time with Petya. Sometimes he puts on a show, especially when he's been drinking. Once, when I was still married, the doorbell rang at two in the morning. Petya, barefoot, in white trousers and a light shirt, stood in the door. Not unusual except that there was snow in the street. He said that his wife was visiting relatives and he was bored and wanted to chat. It was Saturday, no work the next day, and we were happy to see him. He said that he'd been fasting for several days, cleansing his body. Petya was obviously chilled, and my husband suggested a little medicinal alcohol to warm up. As a doctor my husband knew that this was a daring thing—pure alcohol on an empty stomach. Petya gulped back about one hundred grams and followed it with a piece of chocolate. In five minutes he was groggy. He arranged himself in the armchair and said, "Ask me any question, I'll answer anything."

What questions can a Soviet ask? When will this nonsense end and a normal life begin? Especially since this was in Chernenko's time, everyone knew that we were in a ridiculous situation that had to change soon. Petya disappointed us. He said that Chernenko would rule another eight years until his death. "Lucky Chernenko, he'll die soon," Petya said, "but I have another hundred years or more to go. I'm sick and tired of it all."

My husband had his own question: "When will we be allowed out of the country freely?" Petya didn't cheer us up there either. He said it wouldn't be soon and might not ever happen. He was a gloomy forecaster that night.

There was nothing to do but to open the champagne and get drunk like Petya. Once we were tipsy, the conversation perked up. Petya started telling historical jokes. He was very good with ones about Stalin since he could do his Georgian accent very well. Petya went home at five in the morning. Those predictions of his, fortunately, did not come to pass. The poor and ailing Chernenko died soon afterward, and a few years later it was easy to go abroad.

Perestroika suited Petya, and he decided that he could apply his knowledge. Now he works in a joint venture, is greatly respected, and makes a lot of money. He even set up his furniture.

JUNE 12. I've been spending too much time on the "psychos"; I must enjoy them. But it's time to finish up about them. Just one last story, this one about real psychos. Many years ago, in the Brezhnev era, a friend of ours was suffering from insomnia. Nothing—no medicines, not even hypnosis—helped. After much vacillation he decided to go to a hospital. It was almost impossible to get into the division he needed, so a doctor friend said, "If you can stand two days in a critical ward, we'll transfer you to a good one." Aleksandr Nikolayevich had no choice. He came home in three days, cured, so to speak. He never got to the "good ward"; he simply ran like hell from the hospital. A mixture of comedy and tragedy cured him. He was in a real psycho ward. The windows were barred. Knobs were only on the outside of the doors, the lights were on around the clock, and the crazies wandered around all night. But there was democracy and freedom of speech. It was fun watching TV and the official programs. Brezhnev was giving one of his speeches. And what those nuts said to the TV! They swore and cursed, spit at the screen, and threw their slippers at the leader. No one even tried to stop them. What can you expect from a crazy person? For the first time in his life, Aleksandr Nikolayevich felt almost like a free man in a free society. He began doubting that they all were crazy. Then they started playing the Great Patriotic War, as World War II is called in Russia. Aleksandr Nikolayevich's intellectual looks and good manners elicited great respect from the ward's denizens. When they found out that he was a scholar and assistant professor, they unanimously elected him supreme commander and showed him more respect than he ever saw in his lifetime working in a Soviet institute. Aleksandr Nikolayevich sensed that the new life, so to speak, was tempting him, and that was when he ran off. Once he got home, he slept for two days straight, and he almost never suffers from insomnia anymore.

CHAPTER ELEVEN

To America, to America!

JUNE 15. There is a mass exodus from Moscow to the West. All my friends have scattered to Paris, Amsterdam, Rome, and other capitals. I think my turn is coming. This time I'll go farther, cross the ocean. Everyone says that Europe is fine, but it's really good only in America. It's time to get to that promised land at last.

Now I have to gather my remaining strength and prepare for the great battle for tickets, visas, dollars, and other "ingredients" of the trip. I'm glad that I have the invitation in hand, that my American friends have not forgotten me. It's been so long. I really want to go, but at the same time I'm scared. How will things turn out, where will I live, what will I eat? After all, the $320 I'm allowed to exchange rubles for won't last very long. I heard that you're allowed to bring $50 of your own now, so my little savings will come in handy. I have to go to customs and find out what presents you're allowed to bring with you. To tell the truth, I'm not in very good shape. I'm tired of fighting, I don't have the strength. But it's too late to retreat now.

JUNE 18. Today I went to the American Embassy to find out about visas. It's crazy there! Luckily most of the huge crowd has been waiting there for days to get applications for permanent residence. You can receive a guest visa in a day or two, but you have to come early in the morning. There are crowds at all the embassies now, especially the West German one, for many Soviet Germans are going home. It's a very symbolic homeland for the young, who don't even know the language. But they've put up with so much here I can understand their desire to get away. Of course, their eyes are not looking at the poorest country in the world. But it's still a tough deal—strangers in both lands. Here they're called Fascists; there they're considered Communists. Our friend in Berlin has been there for ten years, and people still call her Russian, even though she's pure German. The nurses at the hospital say, "Go to that office, to the Russian doctor." And their families are friends mostly with other former "Russians" because the "real" Germans don't want them too much. But still they are leaving, entire big families, and I would go, too, if I were German.

But I have no other homeland, even though no one seems to needs me here.

This is the wrong mood for travel preparations. The Americans don't give political asylum now, and what if I want to stay?

JUNE 21. So I've been to customs. The picture is pretty grim. There's almost nothing you can take with you. Hanging on the wall there is a long and complicated list of instructions which are almost impossible to understand. I waited my turn and spoke with a stern woman. It feels as if you were being instructed before being put away in prison: no metal objects, nothing that can stab or cut, cigarettes enough until the next time the cart goes by, and so on. Of course, I exaggerate a bit, especially since I'm fortunate enough not to know how you are put into prison. But they talk to you as if you were a potential lawbreaker. You can take only 100 rubles' worth of presents. In other words, you arrive in America and onto the charity of your friends, because you can't go far on $320. Or you could sit on Fifth Avenue with a cup and a sign that says PERESTROIKA, GLASNOST. I'm sure people will give. All those crazy rules are supposed to combat black marketeering, but I know that the real crooks will manage to bring out an elephant if they want.

I came home in a horrible mood, had a fight with Mama over a trifle. I'm very nervous, going off into the unknown.

JUNE 25. It's my own fault. I wanted an adventure, and now I've got to handle it. My Georgian artist friend gave me his painting. He came with his wife to visit me yesterday, learned about my trip, and suggested I take his painting with me. He said that if I'm starving in those "terrible capitalist jungles," I can sell it. It's not a bad deal for him. The painting might fall into good hands. That's how an artist's name is made. He gave me a piece of paper showing that the painting was bought in an art salon.

I called friends who told me that I had to get permission from the Ministry of Culture to take the picture out. I shuddered. Everyone knows what goes on in that place. So I started through the circles of hell. The main office told me that I had to show the painting to a commission that would evaluate it and give permission to take it out of the country. The commission works once or twice a week for a couple of hours, and it's the only one in the whole country. Early in the morning I went off to the address I was given, lugging the heavy and carefully wrapped treasure, only to find an enormous crowd storming a small, dilapidated building in the center of town. You have to sign up in line weeks in advance and check in every week early in the morning. It looks as though I'll be running around checking on my place in lines all over the city. Mama is going to help me. I can't handle it all myself.

JUNE 28. The main thing now is not to spoil my relations with my many friends. People are envious. That's understandable. Who wouldn't want to go to America? No one can believe that I'm in a bad mood, that I'm nervous and want to get into bed and forget about everything. I don't even know where I'll live in New York. I don't have any friends there. Besides, I don't know how I'll buy a ticket to travel beyond New York. Rubles buy a ticket only as far as that city. I have to keep calling America to ask friends to help me, and each call costs up to a hundred rubles. Many naïve women think that over there everything's cheap. One recently told me that almost every public toilet has panty hose for free, in case you get a run and need to change into a new pair. What a Communist future! Everyone is so conscientious and honest and would never take an extra pair. It's amusing to see the utopian propaganda stories the Soviets tell transposed to the "rotten capitalist world." Many friends are offended when I try to return them to reality. They think I'm trying to fool them.

To tell the truth, I myself have only a vague idea of things. I don't know how much things cost, where you can get a cheap meal, or where to shop (I know I'll want to buy something). It's also hard to get used to the idea that what's inexpensive here is expensive there—for instance, the subway and the bus. A ride in the subway in New York is said to cost a dollar, while here it's only five kopecks. And what if you get sick or break a leg, God forbid? Who'll pay for that? Of course, you're better off not landing in a Soviet hospital, but at least it'll kill you for free. As for the famous crime in America, we're well prepared. We have our own.

I wake up at night and wonder, Why the hell am I doing this? I was never afraid to go to Europe. Why am I being so provincial and afraid now? Big deal. They say that America outside New York is just one big village. I'll be fine. I speak the language, my mind's intact, and that seems to be valued there.

JUNE 30.   I got my visa at the embassy today. It wasn't so bad. I came early in the morning, signed up in line, and by twelve was inside the building. The world has changed. Before, our authorities wouldn't let you out of the country. Now it's the Americans who are very careful about letting you into theirs. I've heard they refuse visas to a lot of people. It's a good thing I was warned that you have to answer the questions carefully to create the impression that you're not interested in staying in America. You have to pretend to be happy with your life as a prosperous Soviet citizen: "Yes, my apartment's fine. I like my job; I get a lot of money. I have loads of relatives, and I adore them all. And I'm a patriot and am just going to see how bad things are over there so that I can enjoy it here even more." I think this is crazy, because a person could lie and stay on if he really wanted to. At one point the stupid interrogation drove me to say, "Don't worry, I'm not planning to stay illegally."

At six I was home with the visa. I must admit that the Americans work quickly and well. I had to wait several days at the German Embassy.

JULY 1. At last after enormous efforts I've gained entry with the painting into the dilapidated building. The Ministry of Culture did not disappoint me. It has an inexhaustible supply of surprises. The painting was valued at seven hundred rubles, and now I'll have to pay 100 percent duty at customs—that is, the full amount of seven hundred rubles. The receipt from the art salon says one hundred rubles. The ministry doesn't know that I didn't buy it at all. I showed the receipt and said gloatingly, "I'm so glad the painting has gone up in value. I don't think I'll take it with me. I'll return it to the salon with your new evaluation."

"Our valuation doesn't mean a thing for the salon. We don't guarantee that new price," the ministry girl told me with metal in her voice.

Mama, who helped me in this battle, and I decided to go higher up and find out about these double prices. But as the old saying has it, fish rots from the head. The ladies at the top were even worse and tried to steal the receipt. Mama reacted quickly, tore the piece of paper out of the hand of the more aggressive protector of culture, and left quickly. Curses followed her.

When she got home, Mama called the customs people, who said that the receipt from the art salon was enough. Who's right? We decided that I would take along seven hundred rubles just in case and see what happened.

JULY 3. I think I am going to be a real specialist on lines. It turns out that it's almost impossible to exchange money, too. You have to sign up in line and check in twice a day. Of course, you can find the "right people" and pay them, and they'll do it without a line. The interesting part is that they don't accept rubles for payment, only dollars. The fee is $50, which comes out of your crummy legal $320. I'll fight to the end and won't give that mafia my money. So my number in line is 3,095. The exchange does 300 to 400 a day, so that means close to a week. The crowd is fully democratic or, rather, anarchic. Every day new ideas are tested as our numbers are checked: Write a letter to the Supreme Soviet; declare war on the Mafia. I think we'll soon be called to storm the bank. Of course, the word "storm" makes many people shiver since the Winter Palace was stormed in 1917, and that's why we're all standing in lines.

JULY 4. I got up at six this morning and went to check in at the Aeroflot line and then straight to the bank. Outside Aeroflot everything is in order. There's a respectable and businesslike man in charge. It's like being in the army and he's the commander. But strange things are happening outside the bank. There are several lines at once: the general line, one for people leaving in the next two days, and one for war veterans and invalids. I have a good memory for faces, and yesterday I saw a pushy young man who tried to get into the general line. Today he is on crutches in the line for invalids—a clever and inventive way out. It's time to have a medical commission for that line. I got home at one, took a nap, and went back on watch. I'm cooperating with a young woman. She'll mark me in at Aeroflot, and I'll do the same for her at the bank.

JULY 7. Today is the end of my Aeroflot hassles: I found friends who can help me get a ticket. And I won't have to pay double, in the usual way now. As the saying goes, it's better to have a hundred friends than a hundred rubles. It's a strange life, where money has lost its significance; you can't buy anything with it. Of course, you might try if you have millions, but the only thing our honestly earned hundreds are good for is a couple of trips to the market for vegetables. And people are expected to work hard!

I sometimes think that the best way to survive in our country is to give up all earthly desires and comforts and simply stay in bed and read. Many of my friends are envious of my travels. If they only knew how much effort, time, and health the preparations for these trips can take. I think this one is the record, though.

JULY 10. I feel like a real capitalist; I have $320 in my wallet. If I were to change them at steep black-market rates, I'd have 6,000 rubles or more. I could live for several years without working. It's just a question of how well I'd live. But over there this money will evaporate in just a few days. So how can you explain to an American what a ruble is worth and what it can buy? That's the first thing they ask: How much is it in dollars? When you tell them that a plane ticket from Moscow to Leningrad costs the equivalent of $23, they get confused. The point is that the ruble is worthless. So inside the country there is a currency and prices that have no relation to the rest of the world.

Things went very quickly at the bank. I was almost crushed at the entrance, though. The veterans and invalids decided to push their line forward. I'm terrified of crowds and started screaming and pushing everyone away. I got out with a scare and no broken bones.

It's time to start my own little business—advice for foreign travelers. It will start like this: "Soviet citizens planning to take a private trip abroad must have the following qualities: athletic build, great physical strength to fight off the desperate and angry crowd, iron nerves and inhuman patience for endless lines, inventiveness and quick thinking for instant snap decisions. The absence of the above can be compensated by the presence of several hundred thousand rubles, or even better, a million. The lack of both will make your trip almost impossible. Reading these instructions will be then of no practical benefit. However, for readers in this category, I offer instructions on preparing for preparations for a trip. Recommended time for fulfilling all requirements: one year." I think it sounds good, in the best traditions of Soviet *nomenklatura* literature.

JULY 14. Today is Bastille Day, and I had a great victory, too. I bought or, using Sovietese, I got a plane ticket. It was like a mystery novel. At the appointed hour I came to the courtyard of the building where the airline counters are. I was told to walk around near the yellow door and wait for a young woman in blue jeans and red blouse. Mama was walking in the next little yard, watching through the bushes, just in case (I don't know what case). There was some guy hanging around, too, but we pretended not to notice each other. After twenty minutes I decided I had the wrong door. I found another door and nervously ran between the two of them. No one came out. Then I decided to call. It turned out the girl in jeans had forgotten about it (I'm not giving her name to preserve the conspiracy). Ten minutes later I was in the room. In another fifteen I had a ticket. I counted out the money once more (I had never held so much money at one time before; it was eight months' salary for me) and gave it to the cashier. Hurrah! I couldn't believe it. Moscow–New York–Moscow, leaving in two weeks.

JULY 20. The day of departure approaches, and I'm more and more uncomfortable. Instead of packing, I'm mooching around the apartment, going through useless trifles, gabbing on the phone for hours. And yesterday they did a horrible job at the beauty parlor and I have to go to America looking horrible. I can't decide what clothes to take. Here's good news. I'll be living in a good apartment in midtown Manhattan. But that's the first ten days—and then what?

Katya came by yesterday and said that she'd give half her life to go with me any way she could, in my luggage. Her French fiancé must be gone for good. He hasn't called since he left. If it weren't for the ring on her finger, you'd think she dreamed the whole thing. Now she's ready for the crummiest husband from America. But what can I promise her?

Then Dasha came and told me which New York museums to go to, where to "stretch," and gave me a few phone numbers of American friends. She said that life in Moscow was getting more interesting—new shows, evenings, exhibits, "scenes" but she wouldn't mind going to New York, even though she's not dying of impatience. Her artist seems to have vanished, but she hasn't said anything. Her mood is good. There must be someone new on her horizon. Then the three of us had some French liqueur, Katya and I forgot our anxieties, and Dasha's mood got even better. Maybe I should just booze until I leave. I won't even notice that I'm on the plane? As long as I don't make a mistake and fly to Ulan Bator instead of New York. I'll be put in a mental institution right away if I do that.

JULY 22. People are strange. An acquaintance called and asked what I was planning to bring back to sell. "A computer is best; VCRs are old hat," the practical girl recommended. "Once you sell a computer, you can live without a job for several years and travel around Europe," Larisa went on dreamily.

"Screw the computer, I'm worried about starving over there," I answered angrily.

Larisa explained that the smart people know where to buy and sell. Didn't anyone teach me? No, no one did, but it's too late now. She ruined my mood.

But Larisa is right. That's how everyone travels nowadays; otherwise you won't have enough money for the next trip. You come back, sell the stuff, pay for your next ticket and visa. But a trip to America is a special occasion. I don't mind spending all my savings on it. It's a dream of a lifetime, a trip to the promised land.

What do I actually know about America? I guess quite a bit, but I can't really imagine everyday life. I have tons of clichés in my brain. New York, the capital of the world; California, eternal summer, oranges, Hollywood, Disneyland, earthquakes; Texas, prairies, jeans, cowboys, and JFK was killed there; Alabama, blacks are treated badly there; Kansas, the Wizard of Oz; Washington, the White House, Capitol Hill, the Potomac. I can go on and on, but I'll stop. I also know that Americans are very patriotic about their country, a feeling I don't know very well. Our love for our homeland is a morbid, decadent sorrow. There is almost no pride left.

To tell the truth, what interests me least right now are the stores with their abundance. I've seen stores and have never gone crazy, as actually has happened to a few Soviet tourists.

I've learned to look at stores on my travels as a type of museum of twentieth-century civilization. If you perceive them as real, everyday life, you lose your mind when you go home. After I got back from West Germany, I avoided stores for the first five days, and then things fell into place.

I'm still a bit worried. Will reality correspond to my expectations? When you hear a lot about something, you create your own image of it, often very remote from reality. That happened with the Egyptian pyramids, which seemed much smaller than I had expected. I had thought that one of the Seven Wonders of the World ought to block half the horizon. And now I expect the Statue of Liberty to block my horizon when we approach New York.

JULY 24. I've been packing all my life, and I still can't do it right. I get fits of madness when it takes me a half hour to decide what color scarf or how many pairs of panty hose to pack. When I travel in the USSR, I take absolutely everything with me, including needle, thread, and toothpaste, because you can't buy the most elementary things in other cities. But you can buy everything in America. I just won't have the money. So one more time: six or eight pairs of underwear? Nail polish remover, full or half bottle? Nail polish, red or pink? We're allowed only two suitcases, and I am taking along so many souvenirs, despite the recommendations of the iron customs lady. I feel that I'm about to lose my temper and start swearing out loud, all alone. I'll go to the kitchen instead, have a shot of liqueur, call Dasha, and listen to an update on her boyfriends. I'd love to stick my suitcases in the attic, cancel the trip, get into bed with a book, and stay there for a week. Moscow is a fine city, too. Everyone in the provinces dreams of coming here, and I want to leave the capital of the first socialist country in the world! What's the problem? If I don't like it over there, I'll come right back. A small pleasure for a mere twenty-five hundred. Oh, no, I'll get all I can there. I'll try to see everything. I'm certain that my mood will change the minute I get on the plane. So off to the kitchen to repair my mood.

JULY 26. Friends came by, and we talked a lot about America. There was an unusual program on Radio Liberty recently. It discussed the difference between European and American thinking. Europe lives in the world of ideas, and many don't need to be realized in real life. The idea has its own value. For Americans, the concrete embodiment of the idea is more important. The American is a man of action; the European more of a philosopher, often fruitless. This is my schematic reduction of the argument, but you get the point.

We liked this approach, even though none of us has been in America. We enviously talked about the American sense of obligation and seriousness. Americans say that an oral promise is the same as a written one, that they have respect for their word. Here even a written promise isn't worth the paper it's written on. And people in America work hard, totally immersing themselves in their work. It would be hard for us to do that; we've lost the habit. I wonder if Americans intrigue and squabble at work. To judge from what I've heard from people who've been there, they wouldn't have time. They're all working too hard.

Then we took the other side of the argument and decided that the Russian dreamy inactivity has its charm. Where else can you have a nice friendly chat for hours anyplace at all—at a holiday table, at work, in a line? Time is not money for us, and we feel it very subjectively. If we are in a good mood, we don't hurry; if we are not happy, we try to push time along. We spend half of our lives in a relaxed languor. That's why we're impoverished, of course, and live in tiny apartments and ride buses. But after all, you can't take it with you. In fact, we almost persuaded ourselves that our lives aren't worse, maybe better. I think my friends even felt better about not going to America, which I'm sure they wouldn't mind doing. They left around two. Tomorrow is my last day for packing. I leave early the following day.

JULY 28.   I got on the plane an hour ago, and I still can't calm down. I'm on the verge of total physical exhaustion. Will I find the words to describe it all?

I'll do it in order. Last night, I called a cab to get me at five, so that I could arrive at Sheremetyevo Airport around six in the morning. I had calculated that two hours for check-in would be enough. Some friends came over in the evening. We had a bottle of wine, I cried a bit, but I didn't get a chance to become sad. The friend who had arranged for my ticket phoned and was horrified to hear I had the taxi coming only at five. "You may be at my place for breakfast then," she said ironically.

Then she explained. The airline often oversells seats, and that means people get left behind. Besides, there are often tricky deals going on, so that black-market types get the seats. You can't prove a thing, and before you know it, the plane takes off without you, and you have to spend several days at the airport waiting for another seat.

"Go to the airport around two A.M., and stand by the customs area. When they start registering your flight, you have to be among the first," my friend, wise with experience, told me.

It was pointless going to bed, so we had another bottle of wine (to avoid tension), and I shut my suitcases. I went out into the street, got a cab, and talked the driver (for a lot of money) to take me first to pick up Mama and then to the airport. We were at Sheremetyevo around two.

There's been a lot in the press lately about the scandalous goings-on in the country's main international airport. It made a horrible impression at night. The world's biggest cities were listed on the arrivals and departures boards. You'd think you had one leg in the civilized world, but only one, because the other one didn't even have a place to set itself. The few benches were filled with passengers; some were on blankets on the floor, giving the impression that they lived there. Some went off with toothbrushes and towels to the toilets and returned to go to sleep. Others simply wandered around the airport or tried to sit on their suitcases.

A group of passengers leaving for Vienna—forever—kept to themselves. This was the end of their suffering or maybe the beginning of new torments. But they were in a good mood. Some of the men seemed very aggressive. They tried to persuade us to sign up for a common line into customs and threatened me, saying they wouldn't let me go ahead of them. It was rather amusing, since their flight was at 2:00 P.M. and mine at 8:00 in the morning. We tried to explain that we couldn't let them go first. They shouted and even tried to push us.

This might have been funny, but not at two in the morning, when I was terribly sleepy, my feet hurt, and there was nowhere to sit down. Hot coffee from the thermos we were smart enough to bring helped. We couldn't get near the bar on the first floor. There was a long line, and the barstools were occupied by dozing or sleeping passengers. Mama and I took turns walking around the halls, so as not to fall asleep on the suitcases. It felt like being war refugees. I thought of my warm, cozy bed, just twenty kilometers away. How I'd like to go back home and send America to hell!

For lack of other consolation (and I was already half asleep) I turned to mystical thoughts. This was intended. Fate was taking me through this hard and not understandable path for a reason. I had to accept it and leave it to Providence. I thought of the lines Pasternak gives to Hamlet: "The course of action is planned, the end of the road is predetermined. I am alone, everything drowns in Pharisaism. Living life is not like crossing a field." I have to say that poetry always helps me in difficult moments. I read to myself to relax and get away from reality. The rhythm alone has a magical effect. Besides, we often select the lines that suit our mood and imbue them with our own meaning.

So there I was in the airport at night, weary, uncertain, with expectation and fear. At moments it seemed to me that instead of New York I was headed for Siberia on the last trip. At least that was the mood around me. But the waiting, which seemed an eternity, ended, and the customs agents appeared. On my friend's advice I rushed to be one of the first. You never know. The valiant customs agents decided to demonstrate to the other passengers how well they do their job. "Don't hurry, we've got lots of time," one said to the other.

The execution began. With concentration, unhurriedly, and with sadistic leisure they went through every corner of my suitcases. The thoroughly and carefully packed things turned into a growing pile on the counter. My numerous, I must admit, souvenirs annoyed them. I tried to explain that I had many friends, I would be staying with them, I had to give them something for the hospitality. They'd be feeding me, driving me around; I couldn't even afford to buy myself a sandwich. They knew how much money we're allowed to bring out. "We don't make the laws. And Soviet citizens aren't allowed to speculate abroad," one of the agents said, looking at the five-ruble earrings that wouldn't buy a cup of coffee in America.

This is how the Soviet regime wished me a bon voyage, with accusations and humiliations. But I had no rights, and they could have easily thrown out half my suitcase, citing numerous complicated regulations. Gritting my teeth, I stuffed my things back into the suitcases. But then it was my turn to laugh. An agent saw a jewelry box in my carry-on. "Open the bag, and take out the box." He was expecting a real show—diamond rings and gold bracelets rolling all over the counter. Now I didn't hurry. I took out the box, opened it, and turned it over onto the counter—inexpensive costume jewelry, a wooden bracelet from India covered with yellow metal, fake gold chains, clip-on earrings, and other such stuff. Not believing his eyes, he went through the trifles, hoping to expose me still. The show failed, I think, and his ardor died down. I was allowed to put my things back.

Then came part two—the painting. Here the customs agents were not sure, and to help them, they called in a young woman, a representative of the same glorious Ministry of Culture. In an iron voice I told her that I had a receipt from a salon and that the ministry had told me it was sufficient. My speech was a bit incoherent but convincing. I showed her the stamp the ministry had put on the painting while I was there. The stamp meant that I had been to the commission and that the painting had been valued. I naturally didn't mention its price. So I confused the woman completely and, I think, persuaded her. She was sweet and inexperienced and probably hadn't totally become one of those culture sharks yet. Moreover, I had the sensation that the ministry had one rule and customs another, as often happens here.

Now all I had to do was to stuff everything back in. I was sweating, and my nice clothes for the trip were covered with dust. My desperate attempts were unsuccessful. The things didn't want to go back in. I had to struggle on the floor, since the counter was filled with the belongings of the next victim. So I took out a spare bag and put the overflow into it. I had no idea that this would lead to another fight.

At the ticket and baggage check-in I learned that I had an extra bag and would have pay ninety rubles. The ridiculous part was that once you were past customs you were allowed to have only thirty rubles, which you were supposed to bring back into the country. I thought of the American best seller *Catch-22*. My mother, who was watching all this, managed to get through customs and gave me the money. Ten minutes later my bags were checked in. I went through passport control in a semiconscious state. As I made my way down the hall to the plane, I consoled myself with the fact that I was on my way to New York, not a Stalinist camp. If I had been born earlier, my fate could have been quite different.

Now I'm writing after a pause. After the horrors of the past few hours the plane is heavenly. After a rather edible breakfast for Aeroflot, everyone has quieted down. By the way, breakfast reminds me: I'll never forget the greasy lamb pilaf we got after refueling in Tashkent during a twelve-hour night flight from Sri Lanka. The airline decided to please the passengers with an ethnic dish. You can imagine the reaction to the sight of that greasy food at six in the morning after an almost sleepless night.

The people in the plane are of all different kinds, but I don't think there are any Americans. They prefer the Pan Am flight; it's just eight hours nonstop, compared with our fourteen-hour flight with two stops. There are a lot of Armenian families with decrepit old people and small children, obviously immigrants. They're not afraid to go that far even at their age. Of course, with the situation in the Caucasus being what it is, I can understand them. At least they'll be safe in America. I was told of the inhuman cruelties the Armenians were subjected to by their "Caucasian brothers." They would come into the house, tie up the old people, put an iron on their exposed stomachs, turn it on, and leave. . . . It's hard to believe that people are capable of such things.

The liveliest group is made up of schoolchildren invited by Americans for two weeks. When I was their age, we never even dreamed of such a thing. The only ones to get to America were the children of big bureaucrats. Ordinary people weren't allowed. The privileged kids would come home and behave like conquerors, representatives of a higher Soviet race in blue jeans. I saw a lot of them in college.

A professorial man attracted my attention. He must be going to teach at some university. Half of Moscow's intelligentsia are off at American universities. They are allowed out even with their children. The only problem now is not how to get out of here but how to live there.

I'm writing after yet another break. We had our first stopover in Shannon. It's a different world. Everything is clean. There are lots of little stores with beautiful things and polite, smiling clerks. It's like going from the hell of Sheremetyevo to paradise, yet this is not such a large airport in not the world's richest country. The food on the plane was better, too, tasty and well presented. I'm in a pleasant, dreamy state. We have far to go. The Atlantic lies ahead. I think I'll take a nap.

We've had our second stopover in Canada. I liked the healthy and colorful police. I felt closer to America. One of my romantic American images is the fearless, just, and brave sheriff. I chatted with a Canadian policeman about the strange time zone; it's a half hour off. There are only a few hours left until we reach New York. They'll pass quickly.

And here are the unforgettable and triumphant moments: the announcement that we are coming in for a landing and will be at Kennedy Airport in ten minutes. Everyone's staring out the windows. All we can see is the smooth ocean. To my disappointment, we won't see the Statue of Liberty because we're coming in from the other side. We're very close, but where are the skyscrapers of Manhattan, the ones from my dream? This looks like the suburbs. Won't we even see New York's famous skyline? The plane is on the runway, and the wheels have touched down on the continent of North America. What does it have in store for me? How will my stay in America go? I don't have time to worry about it now. I've gathered my things and will head for the exit—to meet the country I have been dreaming about for so long. Soon there will be new entries in my diary.

Epilogue

After the last lines of this diary were written, great changes occurred in my life and in the life of my country. I got married and now live in California. My husband, Joe, wisely and patiently helps me get used to living in a new land, which is not as easy as it seemed from afar.

Russia beckons as never before. Real hope appeared after the events in August 1991, and people understood that this was the end of enslavement and of the old system, rotten to the core. But it will take many years, perhaps decades, before the country will be rid of the inheritance of the so-called Communist system. I feel a twinge of envy for the young generation, for God willing, their lives will not be distorted and ruined the way ours were and they will not need to go abroad to find freedom. But how do you reimburse those people who did not live long enough to breathe freely, who were destroyed morally or physically by their homeland?

I am grateful to my publisher, Howard Kaminsky, and editor, Maria Guarnaschelli, who found in my diary the value of an ordinary human life and thought it worth publishing. I also express gratitude to my translator, who carefully conveyed the contents and style of the original.

ELENA SUKHORUKIKH ROMINE was born and raised in Moscow where she worked as a guide and interpreter for Intourist. After seven years she went back to University to earn her Ph.D. in philology, leading to a teaching position at the Institute of Advanced Training in Publishing and Journalism in Moscow. In 1989 she made her first trip to the United States and met the man to whom she is now married. Romine lives with her husband in Southern California where she lectures about the latest developments in Russia and the other states comprising the Commonwealth of Independent States.